EVERYTHING I NEED TO KNOW, I LEARNED FROM CARTOONS!

By Art Brown

Copyright © 2011 Art Brown. Renewed 2025
All rights reserved (with the exception of images which fall under the doctrine of "fair use." or so my lawyer tells me)

ISBN 978-1-4357-3248-3

Library of Congress Cataloging-in-Publication Data: Pending

Published by Art of Abundance, Inc. / Callaloo Press

Brooklyn NY and Van Nuys, CA

Printed in the good ol' US of A

Tell me something funny.
Me@ArtBrownProductions.com

DEDICATION

To my Sweetie Trish – who almost always laughs at my jokes.

To my Daughters, Jasmine and Deva – who love me as I am and (more often than not) laugh at my jokes.

To my granddaughter Sitara – Grandpa wrote a book!

To the Men and Women of the animation industry – who benevolently bestowed on us a pernicious plethora of playmates.

To the Great God Television, with its all-powerful cathode rays – which, undoubtedly, have warped my fragile little mind.

And…

To you, dear reader – should you occasionally laugh at my jokes.

INTRODUCTION

I arrived in this world in late January 1959. Dwight D. Eisenhower was President. John F. Kennedy, an ambitious young senator. Buddy Holly, Ritchie Valens and "The Big Bopper" had one week left to make music. There were no personal computers, cellphones, answering machines, microwaves, cable televisions, or iPods. Americans had not yet gone into space, and no–one had ever taken a photo of the earth. There were 49 states in the union, a shameful portion of which was still segregated. The Beatles were perfecting their craft at various Liverpool rave-ups, and no child in America had, as yet requested a Barbie doll.

The predominant form of entertainment in this country (particularly for children) was Television. Manufacturers of cereal, candy and toys knew this well and expended small fortunes to bombard us with lots and lots of commercials. In between those commercials were cartoons.

Since my parents had acquired their television years before I arrived, I looked up to it (and to the characters who resided within it), as to an older sibling. As my parents were usually very busy yelling at each other and planning their divorce, it was only natural that I would reach out to my treasured friends in search of wisdom and guidance.

Following are brief yet loving biographies of my all–wise Kartoon–Karetakers™. After each bio are a few of the unique and timeless lessons which they have so mercifully shared.

Please note that just as every sage does not speak to every seeker, not every cartoon spoke to me. Thus, if I have somehow neglected to celebrate or draw upon one of your personal favorites, my sincere apologies and all I can say is, write your own damn book!

Please also note that my lists and chronologies are in no way meant to be comprehensive. I'm not an encyclopedia – just a humble pilgrim in search of the truth.

So... got a bowl of cereal? All cozy? Great!

In that case kiddies, we now return you to our regularly scheduled program.

TABLE OF CONTENTS

EVERYTHING I NEED TO KNOW, I LEARNED FROM CARTOONS!... 1
    DEDICATION.. 3
    INTRODUCTION 5
    TABLEOF CONTENTS 7
    THE TOONS 10
ALVIN AND THE CHIPMUNKS 10
THE ARCHIE SHOW 11
ASTROBOY 12
BEANY AND CECIL 13
BEETLE BAILEY 15
BETTY BOOP 15
THE BUGS BUNNY SHOW 16
CAP'N CRUNCH 17
CAPTAIN AMERICA 18
CASPER THE FRIENDLY GHOST 19
SONNY THE "CUCKOO FOR COCOA PUFFS" BIRD 20
COURAGEOUS CAT AND MINUTE MOUSE 21
DEPUTY DAWG 21
DICK DASTARDLY (WACKY RACES) 22
DICK TRACY 24
DODO – THE KID FROM OUTER SPACE 25
DUDLEY DO–RIGHT 26
THE EIGHTH MAN 27
FAT ALBERT 28
FELIX THE CAT 29
FLINTSTONES 31
GEORGE OF THE JUNGLE 32
GERALD MC–BOING–BOING 33
GIGANTOR 35
GUMBY AND POKEY 36
HECKLE AND JEKYLL 36
HERCULES 38
HONG–KONG PHOOEY 38
HUCKLEBERRY HOUND 39
THE INCREDIBLE HULK 41
THE INVINCIBLE IRON MAN 41
JOT 42
THE JETSONS 43

THE JETSONS MEET THE FLINTSTONES 44
LUCKY (THE LUCKY CHARMS LEPRECHAUN) 45
MAGILLA GORILLA 46
MIGHTY MOUSE 48
MR. MAGOO 49
PEABODY'S IMPROBABLE HISTORY 50
PEANUTS (CHARLIE BROWN) 51
PETER POTAMUS (AND SO–SO) 52
POPEYE THE SAILOR (Max and Dave Fleischer) 53
POPEYE THE SAILOR (Famous Studios) 56
QUICK DRAW MCGRAW 58
QUISP and QUAKE 60
THE ROAD RUNNER AND COYOTE 60
ROCKY AND BULLWINKLE 61
SECRET SQUIRELL 63
SCOOBY–DOO 64
THE SMURFS 66
SNAP, CRACKLE, POP 68
SNUFFY SMITH 68
SPEED RACER 69
SPIDER MAN 71
PRINCE NAMOR – THE SUBMARINER 73
TENNESEE TUXEDO 74
THE MIGHTY THOR 76
TOM TERRIFIC 77
TOP CAT 78
TOUCAN SAM 79
THE TRIX RABBIT 80
UNDERDOG 81
WALLY GATOR 82
WINKY–DINK AND YOU 83
YOGI BEAR AND BOO–BOO 84
   Latter Day Prophets (Yup, I Still Watch 'Em!) 86
FAIRLY ODD PARENTS 86
FOSTER'S HOME FOR IMAGINARY FRIENDS 87
HOMER, MARGE AND THE KIDDIES 88
POWERPUFF GIRLS 90
REN AND STIMPY 92
SOUTHPARK 93
SPONGEBOB SQUAREPANTS 94
   The Companies 96
DiC ENTERTAINMENT 96
FAMOUS STUDIOS 97
FILMATION 97

Everything I need to know, I learned from Cartoons!   5

FLEISCHER STUDIOS 99
FRED LADD (EARLY ANIMÈ) 104
HANNA–BARBERA 107
JAY WARD PRODUCTIONS 110
KING FEATURES 113
TERRYTOONS 114
TRANS–LUX 118
UPA 119
    CURLY–Q'S™ 124
    INDEX 125

THE TOONS

ALVIN AND THE CHIPMUNKS

The Alvin Show (a.k.a. Alvin and the Chipmunks) had its first run between 1961 and 1962. Had it not been for the hit records, merchandising, and subsequent versions of the show, the characters might have been an animation footnote – as the original run lasted only one season.

The show followed the musical careers, and unorthodox family life of Alvin and his two chipmunk brothers, Theodore and Simon, as they tried the patience of their father figure and manager, Dave Seville.

The Alvin show also introduced us to blowhard professor, Clyde Crashcup and his far more intelligent but mumbling assistant, Leonardo –cartoon precursors to Penn and Teller.

Dave Seville and the chipmunks were created and voiced by Ross Bagdasarian, who had sprung to fame by speeding up voices for his breakout hit, "My Friend the Witchdoctor."

What I Learned:
- *All the coolest kids own either a Harmonica or a Hula Hoop.*
- *Job one for all children is to drive their parents nuts.*

- *In the freewheeling world of show business, all manner of lifestyles are accepted – even cross–species adoption.*
- *You can get away with an amazing amount of nonsense when you're the star.*

THE ARCHIE SHOW

The Archie Show was the first in a long line of Saturday morning cartoons produced by Filmation. Starring those perennial J.D.s from Riverdale, New York, the Archie Show debuted on CBS in September 1968, and appeared in various spinoffs until 1978. Like most Filmation programs, The Archie Show had a laugh track.

The show's most enduring legacy, however, was musical. "The Archies," created and produced by Don Kirshner, and with vocals by Ron Dante and Toni Wine, gave us the hit singles "Sugar, Sugar" (which went to #1 and earned a gold record), as well as their monster hit "Bang shang a lang." Who knew that Veronica could wail like Aretha?

What I Learned:

- *It's possible to drive a car, eat cheeseburgers and even play the drums – all with your eyes closed.*
- *If you're clever enough to sketch a number sign on the side of your head, you can certainly handle two girlfriends.*
- *It's good to be a big fish in a small pond.*

ASTROBOY

Astroboy is the American title for the Japanese animated series "Tetsuwan Atom," which roughly translates as "Mighty Atom," and which was first broadcast on Japanese television in 1963.

Astroboy is set in a future (2003 to be exact), where androids gleefully co–exist with people. Our hero, an android, was created by the head of the Ministry of Science, Dr. Tenma, to replace his son Tobio, who had been killed in a car crash. (This begs the question, what kind of a future is it where children are allowed to drive?) Dr. Tenma tried to love Astroboy like a real son but eventually concluded that love for a robot could not fill his grieving void, so, naturally, Dr. Tenma did what any parent would do in a similar situation. He sold Astroboy to the circus.

That would have been the end of Astroboy, (since, in the future, the circus is nothing more than a depository for unwanted robots), had it not been for Dr. Packadermus J. Elefun, the new head of the Ministry of Science, who discovered Astroboy in the circus and adopted him. Unlike his previous "father," Dr. Elefun treated Astroboy with kindness and respect.

Under Dr. Elefun's gentle guidance, Astroboy became a champion of Japanese justice with an enviable array of powers. To wit:

- Hip–mounted lasers;
- Can translate more than 60 languages;
- Strength equivalent to 100,000 horsepower, allowing him to lift many times his own weight;
- The ability to fly using jets in his feet;
- Magnification of his hearing up to 1,000 times;
- Laser guns deployed at his posterior;
- An electro–heart that can discern people's criminal intentions;
- Bright eye–lamps to assist his vision

What I Learned:

- *Better even than being best pals with a robot, is being the robot.*

- *As the emperor learned with his nightingale, technology alone cannot mend a broken heart.*

- *There's nothing more fun than flying around in your underwear.*

BEANY AND CECIL

Beany and Cecil ran from 1962 to 1967. As the opening theme song makes mind- numbingly clear, the characters were created by Bob Clampett (of Warner Bros fame).

The cartoon followed Beany – a boy, and Cecil– a Sea–Sick Sea Serpent as they sailed around the world with Captain Horatio Huffenpuff, also called "Uncle Captain," on his ship, "the Leakin' Lena."

Beany, as his name suggests, wore a "beanie" hat with a propeller. This remarkable chapeau enabled the lad to fly.

Often, Beany would be kidnapped by the villain (Dishonest John), and cry "Help, Cecil! Help, help!" to which Cecil would reply "I'm comin', Beany–boy!" as he raced to the rescue.

Cecil, whose tail was never seen, was fiercely loyal to Beany, although he was not the brightest monster in the loch. Cecil's tail never being seen was a sort of "in joke," as a hand–puppet version of Beany and Cecil had predated the cartoon.

Dishonest John, the villain of the story, dressed like Simon Legree, and schemed to ruin Beany and Cecil's wholesome fun. His catchphrase was a sinister "Nya ha ha!"

What I Learned:

- *When your first name is "dishonest," people are bound to judge you.*
- *Anyone can fly – with the proper headgear.*
- *Sock puppets and mythical sea serpents are our friends.*

BEETLE BAILEY

Although Beetle Bailey has been a private in the U.S. Army since 1950, he has quite remarkably never in all that time been sent into combat. Stationed at Camp Swampy in the longest ever period of basic training, he goofs off as much as possible, endures a sadomasochistic relationship with his sergeant (Sergeant Snorkel), and never lifts his hat above his eyes. Well, almost never. The one and only time Beetle ever removed his hat was in a 1960s Mad Magazine parody. On his forehead was written, "Get out of Vietnam."

In 1963, King Features incorporated Beetle into a trilogy of made for TV cartoons, which also included Snuffy Smith and Krazy Kat.

What I Learned:
  Particularly in times of danger or war, be a slacker. You'll probably live longer.

BETTY BOOP

Betty Boop, flapper extraordinaire, came into this world as a dog. Created as a girlfriend for canine character, Bimbo, Max Fleischer and his brother Dave, (wanting to avoid being seen as promoting interspecies dating), initially endowed our Betty with dog-ears and a tail. The Fleischers soon caught wise that sex trumps cute and made her all-woman. In addition, the fact that Fleischer's studio was in New York city (46th street and Broadway), gave the shorts a distinctly urban feel and made it convenient for many of the early jazz greats to play on his cartoons. As a result, Fleischer was able to produce the timeless Betty shorts, "Minnie the Moocher," and "I'll be glad when you're dead, you rascal you," featuring Cab Calloway and Louis Armstrong respectively.

What I Learned:

- *Don't let them take your "boop, boop a doop" away. If you're fortunate enough to discover what's special, unique and precious about you, hold on to it for dear life, and don't ever let the "Sideshow Ringmasters" talk you out of it.*

- *Sex sells – especially to precocious children.*

THE BUGS BUNNY SHOW

The Bugs Bunny Show was a long-running anthology series hosted by Bugs, which was mainly comprised of Looney Tunes and Merrie Melodies cartoons originally created in the 1940s and 50s. The show originally debuted as a primetime ABC program in 1960, with newly produced wraparound segments done by the Warner Bros. animation staff, including Chuck Jones, Friz Freleng, and Robert McKimson. The wraparounds were produced in color, but the original broadcasts of the show were in black–and–white.

This show is credited with keeping the Golden Age Warner Bros. cartoons alive. Indeed, the show ran for more than four decades, and helped inspire animators, comedians, historians, and just about anyone who was a fan of "Termite Terrace" (the nickname Warner animators had given their division).

What I Learned:

- *Annoy your enemies as much as possible. They will eventually throw down their guns and start crying.*

- *Always have a spare rabbit hole to dive into.*

- *Sang–froid baby, sang–froid.*

CAP'N CRUNCH

For nearly five decades, TV commercials have made **Cap'n Crunch** a Saturday morning icon. When Cap'n Crunch commercials debuted, they featured three children and their dog who sailed with the Cap'n on his ship, The Good Ship Guppy, ever encountering the Cap'n's nemesis, Jean LaFoote, the "barefoot pirate." The Cap'n Crunch cereal boxes contained small comic books featuring these characters.

These commercials were in fact mini–cartoons, produced by Jay Ward productions (famous for Bullwinkle), and containing the same off-beat humor. Daws Butler would provide the voice of the Cap'n from the 1960s until his death in 1988.

What I Learned:

- *A key player in the Battle of New Orleans was Jean LaFoote.*
- *The most valuable things on earth are Crunchberries.*

CAPTAIN AMERICA

One of a series of cartoons made by the "Merry Marvel Marching Society"(Marvel Comics) in 1966, **Captain America** provided good old patriotic crime fighting during the turbulent and morally ambiguous 1960s. The good Cap acquired his powers during World War II, through an army sponsored experiment to create a super soldier who could better fight the Nazis. His chief enemy at that time was a Nazi agent named "the Red Skull."

Other cartoons in the series included "The Mighty Thor," "The Incredible Hulk," "The Submariner," and "Iron Man."

What I Learned:

- *With a little practice, a large metallic Frisbee can be used as a weapon.*

CASPER THE FRIENDLY GHOST

Casper the friendly Ghost was created in the early 1940s by Seymour Reit and Joe Oriolo, the former devising the idea for the character and the latter providing illustrations. Oriolo eventually sold the rights to Paramount Pictures' Famous Studios, for which he occasionally worked.

"The Friendly Ghost," the first Noveltoon to feature Casper, was released by Paramount in 1945. In the cartoon, Casper is a pudgy little ghost–child, who prefers making friends to scaring people. Consequently, he flees his haunted home in search of playmates. However, every person or animal he meets takes one horrified look at him and runs away. Despondent, Casper tries to commit suicide, apparently forgetting that he's *already dead*. Just when he's about to give up, he meets two little children who accept him. Naturally, the children's mother at first rejects Casper as an unsuitable playmate, but she later welcomes him into the family after he frightens off the landlord.

Nearly every cartoon had the same plot: Casper rejects the life of a "normal" ghost, tries to find friends, scares nearly everyone, prompting them to run away while screaming, "It's a g–g–g–ghost!!" and finally meets a cute little child or animal whom he saves from some sort of trouble, thus creating, at long last, a friend – that is until the next cartoon, when he's lonely again.

Casper was voiced by the late Norma MacMillan, who also voiced Underdog's Sweet Polly Purebred as well as Gumby.

What I Learned:
- ***There is definitely life after death – but once you cross over, there's little point in coming back and trying to get people to like you.***

SONNY THE "CUCKOO FOR COCOA PUFFS" BIRD

Sonny the Cuckoo Bird was the mascot for Cocoa Puffs. In the commercials, Sonny would attempt to focus on a sober, non–cocoa–puffs related task. Unfortunately, the world we live in is chockablock with Cocoa goodness. Consequently, Sonny is confronted by some reference to or reminder of his Cocoalistic obsession. This blows his mind and he freaks out, bouncing off the walls and yelling, "I'm cuckoo for Cocoa Puffs!"

If only these commercials had been seen by my generation as the cautionary tales that they were...

What I Learned:
- ***If you act crazy enough, they'll give you cereal.***
- ***Before Prozac or Wellbutrin– there were Cocoa Puffs.***
- ***In the words of Oscar Wilde, "the surest way to get rid of a temptation is to yield to it."***

COURAGEOUS CAT AND MINUTE MOUSE

Courageous Cat and Minute Mouse were created by Bob Kane as a parody of, and a way to further cash–in on, his earlier and far more famous characters: Batman and Robin. Courageous Cat and Minute Mouse thwarted criminals by using their all– purpose Catgun and chasing evildoers in their Catmobile. They also fought crime out of a Cat–cave. Basically, if you change the "B" to a "C" in every single scenario… well you get the idea. Their arch–enemy was The Frog, whose character and voice were based on liver–lipped tough guy, Edward G. Robinson.

What I Learned:

- *Who knew there were guns that shoot ropes?*

- *Cats and mice can and should look out for each other, but frogs are just evil.*

DEPUTY DAWG

As indicated by his title, **Deputy Dawg** proudly served his community in the capacity of deputy sheriff. He lived in a region of the country where words like "dog" are drawled – specifically, backwoods Mississippi. The Deputy's "friends" (including Ty Coon, Muskie the

Muskrat and Vincent Van Gopher), rarely had the good Deputy's best interests in mind, and frequently had to be chased from either the local chicken coop or watermelon patch. The sheriff of the town (one rank above our hero) was a white-mustached human, who harassed Deputy Dawg from above just as his fellow animals harangued him from below.

Most of the voices were done by Dayton Allen (who also did both Heckle and Jekyll), but Lionel Wilson (Sidney the Elephant, and Tom Terrific) handled some of the incidental characters.

What I Learned:

- *Muskrats love watermelon and are much smarter than dawgs.*
- *Some portions of rural America are so impoverished, that they cannot afford human workers and must hire animals.*
- *Vincent Van Gogh wore a beret and was blind.*

DICK DASTARDLY (WACKY RACES)

Dick Dastardly, (voiced by the inimitable Paul Winchell) was the evil protagonist of that groovy 1960s car show, "Wacky Races." His chief competitors in this never-ending contest were:

- The Slag Brothers in the Bouldermobile
- The Gruesome Twosome in the Creepy Coupe
- Professor Pat Pending in the Ring-a-Ding Convert-a-Car
- Red Max in the Crimson Haybailer
- Penelope Pitstop in the Compact Pussycat

- Sergeant Blast and Private Meekly in the Army Surplus Special
- The Ant Hill Mob in the Bulletproof Bomb
- Luke and Blubber Bear in the Arkansas Chuggabug
- Peter Perfect in the Turbo Terrific
- Rufus Ruffcut and Sawtooth in the Buzz Wagon

Dastardly drove "The Mean Machine," which featured all sorts of devices for him to use against his opponents. As Wacky Races was inspired by the film "The Great Race," so was Dastardly derived from the movie's chief villain, Professor Fate. Dastardly wore old-fashioned racer's gear — a long violet overcoat, long red gloves, and a large striped hat with driving goggles attached. Dastardly, like his peer Snidely Whiplash, sported a luxurious handlebar mustache.

Dastardly was aided in his schemes by his sidekick, a scruffy dog named Muttley who had a distinctive wheezy laugh.

Dick Dastardly continued his villainous career in the Wacky Races spin-off "Dastardly and Muttley in their Flying Machines," also known as "Stop That Pigeon!" (due to the theme song's repeated use of that phrase).

What I Learned:

- *Neanderthals make excellent drivers, when they're not hitting each other with clubs.*
- *Squinty-eyed men with handlebar moustaches are frequently up to no good.*
- *For some people, applying your makeup correctly is much more important than winning a race.*

DICK TRACY

Dick Tracy, created by Chester Gould, first appeared in the funny- papers in 1931. The realistic police- action strip chronicled the adventures of Tracy, a square-jawed detective, in his battle against misshapen criminals. His popularity inspired a radio show, movie serials, a 1950's live action TV show, and finally in 1961, cartoons.

Production began on the cartoons in 1960. They added several supporting characters to the cast including Heap O' Calorie (patterned after actor Andy Devine), Hemlock Holmes (Cary Grant), The Retouchable Squad (a Keystone Kops-like group whose name parodied the Untouchables), and two characters who would now be considered politically incorrect due to their portrayal of racial stereotypes: Jo Jitsu, an Oriental master of martial arts, and Go-Go Gomez, a Mexican gumshoe who was a master of disguises. In the first season, the voice of Go-Go Gomez was done by Mel Blanc.

A few of the master criminals this team of super-cops battled were Sketch Paree, The Mole, Flattop, B. B. Eyes, Mumbles, The Brow, Noodles, Pruneface, and Itchy.

What I Learned:

- *When beating the tar out of your enemy, above all, be polite.*
- *You can talk to people through your wrist-watch, and they will talk back.*

- *A small person, (or a kid), can overpower a big person through a simple mastery of Jui Jitsu.*
- *Crime does not pay – unless your name is Halliburton.*

DODO – THE KID FROM OUTER SPACE

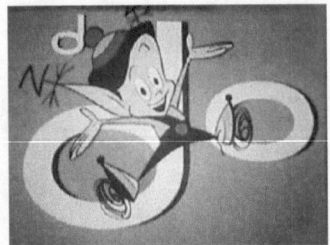

DoDo–The Kid from Outer Space was produced in 1964 and released into U.S. syndication in 1965, airing on stations such as KHJ, Los Angeles. DoDo gained its greatest U.S. exposure from 1966 through 1970 during a run on many NBC affiliates. The animation style of DoDo resembled popular Japanese cartoons of the same era, such as Astroboy and Speed Racer, but was actually produced by Hungarian–born John Halas and his wife Joy Batchelor, British animators best known for the 1954 feature–length animated version of George Orwell's Animal Farm. Halas & Batchelor later animated The Osmonds and The Jackson 5ive for Rankin–Bass as well as The Addams Family and The Partridge Family: 2200 A.D. for Hanna–Barbera.

DoDo was a young alien child with long pointy ears who wore overalls. He had little whirling propellers on his heels which enabled him to fly, and he came from the "atomic" planet Hena Hydro. He traveled around with his pet bird, "Compy" (who was part computer, and who was born when Compy's mother laid an egg on top of computerized punch cards).

DoDo and Compy spent their days encountering Earthlings and learning their "strange" Earth ways. They were assisted by one of Hena Hydro's foremost researchers, Professor Fingers, a tall, skinny, balding man whose research delved into unresolved mysteries.

Professor Fingers had inter–dimensional pockets, which enabled him to fit objects of any size into his lab coat.

What I Learned:
- *Scientific inquiry and anonymity do not always go hand in hand.*
- *Take care where your pet bird lays her eggs.*

DUDLEY DO–RIGHT

Dudley Do–Right was the hero of a segment on The Rocky & Bullwinkle Show which parodied early 20th century melodrama and silent film cliffhangers. Dudley was a Canadian Mountie who was always trying to catch his nemesis Snidely Whiplash, usually without success. His love interest was Nell Fenwick, the daughter of the chief of the Mounties. Unfortunately, Nell was far more attracted to Dudley's horse.

What I Learned:
- *People will greatly admire you if you can gallop backwards on a horse.*
- *True evil doers are anemic, frequently with a tinge of green.*

- *There's some very weird stuff going on between girls and ponies.*

THE EIGHTH MAN

After detective Brady is murdered by the evil Saucer Lip, Brady's mind and soul are transferred to a super android by the aptly named Professor Genius. Dubbed "Tobor" (spell it backwards), the Eighth Man by the Professor, he resumed the chase for his killer, operating out of the Metropolitan International Police Headquarters. Only Chief Fumblethumbs knew his secret identity. When Tobor needed extra power, he smoked a radioactive cigarette!

By the time Professor Genius created Eighth Man he had been unsuccessful with seven previous robots. During that period, he was only known as "Professor Very, Very Smart."

Like much animé, **Eighth Man** dealt with many adult themes, such as murder and death, in a very direct manner. Also, had it not been for "the Eighth Man," we might never have been exposed to that scintillating hit of the 1970s, "the Six–Million Dollar Man."

What I Learned:
- *Smoking is a bad idea for people, but just fine for super-robots.*

FAT ALBERT

Fat Albert first appeared as a character in Bill Cosby's stand-up act and on his 1967 album "Revenge." The stories were based on Cosby's tales of growing up in Philadelphia. In 1969, Cosby and veteran animator Ken Mundie brought Fat Albert to the small screen in a one-shot prime-time special entitled "Hey, Hey, Hey, It's Fat Albert."

The special, which aired on NBC, was a hybrid of live-action and animation. The music for the special (and later the series) was written and performed by jazz pianist Herbie Hancock and later released as the Warner Bros. album "Fat Albert Rotunda."

Next, the producers attempted to bring Fat Albert to Saturday mornings, but NBC refused because they felt the series was too educational. So, Bill Cosby and Filmation, took the property to CBS.

Fat Albert indeed was famous for its educational content. During each episode, Fat Albert and his friends, collectively known as The Junkyard Gang, dealt with an issue or problem commonly faced by young children, ranging from stage fright, first loves ("puppy love"), medical operations, or skipping school, to harder, more serious themes (toned down somewhat for young children) including smoking, stealing, racism, being scammed by con artists, child abuse, drug use, and gun violence.

At the end of each episode, the gang would grab various pieces of garbage that they'd found in the junkyard and sing a song about the theme of the day.

Other members of the gang included Mushmouth, Dumb Donald, and Weird Harold.

What I Learned:
- *Childhood obesity? Crushing poverty? They are not obstacles, but opportunities.*
- *There's room in this wide world for everyone, regardless of their size or speech impediment.*

FELIX THE CAT

Felix the Cat was the most popular cartoon character in silent–films. His black body, white eyes, and giant grin, coupled with the surrealism of the situations in which he was placed, combined to make Felix one of the most recognizable cartoon characters in the world. Felix was the first character from animation to attain a level of popularity sufficient to draw movie audiences based solely on his star power.

Felix's origins remain disputed. Australian cartoonist and film entrepreneur Pat Sullivan and American animator Otto Messmer both claimed to be his creator, and evidence seems to back up both claims. However, many historians, such as John

Canemaker, argue that Messmer ghosted for Sullivan. Other historians disagree. What is certain is that the cat emerged from Sullivan's studio.

During the 1920s, Felix enjoyed enormous popularity around the world. He got his own comic strip (drawn by Messmer), and his image adorned all sorts of merchandise. Jazz bands such as Paul Whiteman's sang about him. Nevertheless, the success was short–lived. The arrival of talking cartoons, particularly those of Walt Disney's Mickey Mouse, eclipsed the silent offerings of Sullivan and Messmer. A few talking Felix shorts failed to win back audiences.

Television would prove the cat's savior. Felix cartoons began airing on American TV beginning in 1953. Meanwhile, Joe Oriolo, the new artist behind the Felix comic strip, gained the rights to feature Felix in a new series specifically for television. Oriolo introduced new characters, such as Poindexter, The Professor, and Rock Bottom, and he gave Felix a "Magic Bag of Tricks," which could shift into myriad shapes based on Felix's needs. Joe Oriolo's son, Don Oriolo, continues as Felix's caretaker today, and the cat has since starred in other television programs and in a feature film.

Many of the characters, including Poindexter and The Professor were voiced by Jack Mercer – for 60 years, the voice of Popeye.

What I Learned:

- ***Be prepared for any dilemma – even if you have to use magic.***

◈ *Someone can be trying to kill you one moment and be your greatest ally the next. Don't let it confuse you.*

◈ *It feels great to throw your entire body back and laugh from your toes.*

FLINTSTONES

The Flintstones takes place in a town called Bedrock in the Stone Age. Everything is a corollary to 1950s America, but "prehistoric." The characters drive automobiles made out of stone or wood and animal skins and which are powered by their feet. In our prehistoric past, extremely powerful feet were of paramount importance.

One of the show's running gags was the way animals were used for technology. For example, when the characters took photographs with an instant camera, the inside of the camera box would be shown to contain a bird carving the picture on a stone tablet with its beak. The animal powering such technology would break the fourth wall, look directly at the audience, and drone, "It's a living."

The series drew directly from "The Honeymooners" for its main quartet of characters: the bombastic Fred Flintstone and his wife Wilma (modeled after the Kramdens), and their neighbors Barney and Betty Rubble (modeled after the Nortons). Later additions to the cast included the Flintstones' infant daughter Pebbles and the Rubbles' abnormally strong adopted son Bamm–Bamm. The Flintstones also had a pet dinosaur named Dino which barked like a dog, while the Rubbles had a pet kangaroo named Hoppy.

What I Learned:

- *When bowling, approach the lane on your tiptoes.*
- *A big enough side of ribs can tip your car over.*
- *Even if you never, ever, ever have a housecat, you still need to put him out for the night.*
- *Who needs brakes, when you have feet?*

GEORGE OF THE JUNGLE

George of the Jungle was originally broadcast on ABC in 1967. A parody of Tarzan, the series was produced by Jay Ward and Bill Scott, who were also responsible for Rocky and Bullwinkle.

The title character, voiced by Scott, was a dim–witted but big–hearted "ape man," who lived in the jungle and was called upon each episode to save its inhabitants from danger. Among other things, George was well–known for becoming distracted while vine–swinging, thus slamming face–first into trees.

George's posse included his girlfriend "Ursula" (voiced by June Foray), his gorilla friend "Ape" (voiced by Paul Frees), who is far more intelligent than George (and sounds like Ronald Colman); and his pet elephant, "Shep," who behaves like a lap dog. Appropriately, George refers to Shep as his "great big peanut–luvin poochie." Rarely seen in the show, but mentioned in the theme song is "Fella," which is how George refers to the "second" Ursula who appears to him when he hits his head too hard and sees double. Other notable wildlife includes the Tooky–Tooky bird renowned for its strident call: "ah ah ee ee tooky tooky."

What I Learned:

- *Evolution is a scientific fact, but in which direction?*
- *Don't be afraid to have team–mates who are smarter than you.*
- *If you happen to swing face–first into a tree, you will suffer no consequences.*

GERALD MC–BOING–BOING

Gerald McBoing–Boing was originally a one–shot cartoon released in 1950 by UPA. It won the Oscar for best short that same year.

Gerald McBoing–Boing is the story of a little boy who speaks through sound effects instead of spoken words, and how this misfit eventually makes his talents work for him. It was adapted from a story by Dr. Seuss – and you can hear that great Seuss poetry in the narrative. The film has been selected for preservation in the United States National Film Registry. In 1994, it was voted #9 of the 50

Greatest Cartoons of all time by members of the animation field.

This film was the first successful theatrical cartoon produced by United Productions of America (UPA), after their initial experiments with a short series of cartoons featuring Columbia Pictures stalwarts the Fox and the Crow. It was meant to be an artistic attempt to break away from the strict realism in animation that had been developed and perfected by Walt Disney. While Disney's animation methods produced lush and awe–inspiring images, it was felt that realism in the medium of animation was a limiting factor. Cartoons did not have to obey the rules of the real world (as the short films of Tex Avery and their cartoon physics proved), and so UPA experimented with a non–realistic style that depicted caricatures rather than lifelike representations of real people.

This was a major step in the development of limited animation—though despite the abuse of the form that would arise in the future (due to cost–cutting methods), Gerald McBoing–Boing was meant as an artistic exercise rather than merely a way of producing cheap cartoons.

UPA produced three follow–up McBoing–Boing shorts: Gerald McBoing–Boing's Symphony (1953), How Now Boing Boing (1954), and Gerald McBoing–Boing on the Planet Moo (1956), an Academy Award nominee. The second and third films maintained the Dr. Seuss–style rhyming narration but were not based on his work. The final film abandoned this approach.

What I Learned:

- ❷ *When in public, make lots of strange noises. If nothing else, it will get you a seat on the subway.*

- ❷ *Stand firm in your weirdness. Sooner or later the world will rally around your oddities and pay.*

GIGANTOR

Gigantor was a rocket–propelled flying robot with a Pinocchio–like nose. He was controlled by twelve year old boy Jimmy Sparks. Gigantor was invented by Dr. Bob Brilliant, Jimmy's scientist father, to assist Inspector Blooper and the Japanese police in their war against crime. The characters were first seen in Japanese "manga" comics, and brought to life by Fred Ladd, who also worked on the American version of Astroboy and Eighth Man. I wonder how they'd resolve it were both Dr. Brilliant and Professor Genius (of Eighth Man) to reach for the same chicken wing at a party.

What I Learned:

- ❷ *12 year old boys and humungous robots are natural allies.*

GUMBY AND POKEY

Gumby was the boyish green hero of a strange claymation world which aired for 223 episodes over a period of 35 years. His side–kick and confidant was Pokey, a red claymation horse. Just as with all true hipsters, Gumby and Pokey constantly fought against the squares (or in their case, the "Block–heads").

Created by claymation pioneer, Art Clokey, Gumby had its genesis in a 1955 theatrical short called Gumbasia, which featured similar claymation characters. For the series, Art Clokey provided the voice of Pokey. Later, Clokey also created the doctrinaire religious show, "Davey and Goliath," in partnership with the Lutheran church.

Rumors have long persisted that Art was an early follower of Timothy Leary, and hence a psychedelic traveler. The world of Gumby offers nothing to dispute that claim.

What I Learned:
● ***This IS my brain on drugs.***

HECKLE AND JEKYLL

Heckle and Jekyll was originally a theatrical cartoon series created and released by Terrytoons. The characters were a pair of identical magpies who calmly outwitted their foes like Bugs Bunny, while creating random mischief like Woody Woodpecker.

One magpie spoke with a British accent, while the other talked like a Nu–Yawker, although it was always uncertain which character was which. Some say that Jekyll was the British one, perhaps by association with the British surname "Jekyll," coupled with the assumption that a New Yorker might be more likely to "heckle" people.

In attempting to resolve this question, I reached out to animation great, Gene Deitch, who at one time ran Terrytoons. His erudite and measured response was simply, "the one with the beak is Heckle, and the one with the black feathers is Jekyll." Thanks Gene.

The magpie is a frequent symbol in European folklore. Generally speaking, the bird is associated with unhappiness and trouble. This may be because of its well-known tendency to "steal" shiny objects, as well as its harsh, chittering call.

An old English folk tale states that when Jesus was crucified, all of the world's birds wept and sang to comfort him in his agony. The only exception was the magpie, and for this, it is forever cursed.

In Scottish folklore, (in a story possibly related to the above) magpies were long reviled for allegedly carrying a drop of Satan's blood under their tongues.

What I Learned:

๑ *Many birds, particularly magpies, are approximately the same size as an angry farmer, or a very stupid dog.*

HERCULES

Recasting ancient strongman **Hercules** as one more Superman wannabe, the folks at Trans–Lux created an action–packed, limited animation, adventure series. Equipping him with a magic ring and a stammering side–kick, Hercules helped the people of ancient Greece whenever they were in trouble.

What I Learned:

๑ *The ancient Greek Gods looked and behaved very much like characters from DC comics.*

๑ *Mythical fauns tend to stutter.*

HONG–KONG PHOOEY

A somewhat inept super–hero, **Hong Kong Phooey** was a self–proclaimed master of kung fu and other martial arts. Always on the alert for crime, he got his tip–offs from the police station where he worked as Penrod "Penry" Pooch, the mild mannered janitor. Whenever Penry heard of a crime taking place, he leapt into a filing cabinet where he changed into his crime fighting gear. Unfortunately, he usually got stuck there and needed the help of his loyal cat Spot to get out.

Hong Kong Phooey would travel from crime scene to crime scene in his ever adapting Kung Fu car. One "bong of the gong" and the Phooeymobile would instantly change into a plane, a boat, a snowmobile, or whatever was needed to save the day.

Hong Kong Phooey was based on the distinctive voice and personality of actor Scatman Crothers.

What I Learned:

  ◙ *Multiculturism works. The gorgeous mosaic is a success. Even a scat–singing beagle can master karate.*

  ◙ *Cats are smarter than dogs, or at least far more practical.*

HUCKLEBERRY HOUND

The Huckleberry Hound Show was William Hanna and Joseph Barbera's second made–for–TV series ("The Ruff and Reddy Show," NBC–TV 1957–60 was their first.) The series premiered in 1958 and starred a good–natured hound dog with a Southern drawl. Sponsored nationally by Kellogg's Cereals, the show was the first fully animated series made exclusively for television. With a budget of about $2,800 per episode, Hanna and Barbera invented a technique called "limited animation." This process greatly reduced the number of drawings needed to complete a single cartoon, which allowed them to stay within budget and dominate the ratings for the next three decades.

Huckleberry Hound was the tale (tail) of an easy going dog meandering through life from job to job and situation to situation – taking life as it is, then moving on; kind of like a cartoon distillation of Kerouac's "The Dharma Bums."

In the premiere episode, "Wee Willie," Police officer Huckleberry is assigned the difficult task of returning a playful escaped gorilla to the zoo. Subsequent episodes revealed Huck pursuing such varied occupations as mailman, truant officer, veterinarian, lion tamer, explorer, mounted police officer, firefighter, and even the improbable career of dogcatcher.

Huckleberry's relaxed Southern accent was provided by the late, great Daws Butler. Many episodes began with Huck ambling along attempting to sing, "My darling clementine."

Like many cartoons of the time, Huckleberry Hound was particularly unabashed in its promotion of the sponsor's products. Consequently, this series is a significant factor in the now well-established bond between Cartoons and Cereal.

What I Learned:
- *You can speak slowly, have a kindly demeanor, comport yourself in an exceedingly humble fashion, and still be an effective leader.*
- *Don't worry. Be happy.*
- *Based solely on complexion, Huckleberry Hound is a direct descendent of Krishna.*

THE INCREDIBLE HULK

One of a series of cartoons made by the "Merry Marvel Marching Society" (Marvel Comics) in 1966, **The Incredible Hulk** was born when Dr. Bruce Banner got in the way of some Gamma rays. For the 1970s TV series featuring Bill Bixby and Lou Ferrigno, the writers changed his first name to David, perhaps thinking that the name "Bruce" sounded "too gay."

Other cartoons in the series included, "Captain America," "The Mighty Thor," The Submariner, and "Iron Man."

Don't get him angry. You wouldn't like him when he's angry."

What I Learned:
* *Treat everyone you meet with kindness and respect – especially that unassuming scientist.*

THE INVINCIBLE IRON MAN

One of a series of cartoons made by the "Merry Marvel Marching Society" (Marvel Comics) in the late 1960s, **The Invincible Iron Man** is the only superhero whose comic book origin stems from the Vietnam war. Ambushed by the Viet Cong, Tony Stark found himself a prisoner with a piece of shrapnel lodged near his heart. To stay alive and to break free of his Vietcong captors, he invented his miraculous suit of iron. Originally, Tony could not ever remove the armor or the shrapnel would travel to his heart and he would die. That conceit was modified when Iron Man became a series.

Other cartoons in the series included, "The Mighty Thor," "The Incredible Hulk," "The Submariner," and "Captain America."

Iron Man's alter–ego, millionaire playboy and industrialist, Tony Stark, always reminded me of someone... also a superhero... also a millionaire playboy... lived in stately Wayne manor. Hmmm... can't think of it.

What I Learned:
- **People with defective (or broken) hearts need to wear lots of armor.**

JOT

JOT was a series of unintentionally macabre cartoons produced by the Southern Baptist Radio and Television Commission (RATC). These five–minute morality plays were created to teach children about religion but instead wound up scaring the living bejeezus out of them.

The cartoons have a minimalist, UPA influenced look combined with a good deal of psychedelic imagery.

The main character, JOT, is a white circle with occasional hands and feet (his limbs only appeared when he was moving). JOT's name is a reference to Matthew 5:18, "For verily I say unto you, till heaven and earth pass, one jot or one tittle shall in no wise pass from the law, till all be fulfilled." Too bad they didn't name this show, "Tittle."

Production began in 1959, with the first episode released in 1965. The series premiered on Peppermint Place, a Sunday children's show produced locally at KFAA in Fort Worth, Texas. The episodes were eventually syndicated throughout the world and translated into 19 different languages. Lucky us.

What I Learned:
● *Don't eat that cupcake or you'll roast in hell.*

THE JETSONS

George Jetson worked 3 hours a day, 3 days a week for a short, tyrannical boss named Cosmo G. Spacely, owner of Spacely Sprockets, who was voiced by the incomparable Mel Blanc. (Listen to Mr. Spacely yelling, "Jetson! You're fired!" followed by Daffy intoning, "you're despicable.") George commuted to work in a tiny flying saucer and his day consisted of pressing a single computer button, which began the Spacely Sprocket machinery.

Daily life afforded an abundance of leisure time due to the advances in automation. Despite this, the Jetsons often griped about the trials of modern living.

Other members of the Jetson clan included Jane Jetson, the wife and homemaker; teenage daughter Judy, and preteen son

Elroy. Housekeeping was seen to by a robot maid, Rosie. The family dog Astro could mutter phrases such as "Ruh–roh!" and "Right, Reorge!" (not unlike Scooby–Doo and Muttley). Don Messick did the voices for all of them.

In the Jetsons' world, all homes and businesses were raised high above the ground on narrow poles, ostensibly to escape from the smog. In fact, the Jetsons' architecture reflected a real world school of architecture known as "Googie." This futuristic style can be seen at Disneyworld's Tomorrowland as well as the Seattle Space Needle and various structures nationwide.

What I Learned:

- *In the future, we will work less, have talking dogs and live high above the smog.*
- *We will have wild rock and roll parties and dance on the ceiling.*
- *"Eep Opp Ork Ah ah" will still mean, "I love you."*

THE JETSONS MEET THE FLINTSTONES

The Plot: Elroy invents a time machine, which goes "kablooey," sending the entire **Jetson** family back to the stone–age – where they naturally meet up with the **Flintstones**. Then, everyone gets sent "back to the future" (years before Marty McFly). Some fun!

What I Learned:

- *In the very near future, although we will have flying cars and robot maids, most people will still be afraid of their bosses. In the distant past, although cavemen had cars, televisions, telephones and elephants to give them showers, they still argued with their spouses. While fashions may come and go, the essential nature of the human heart abides.*

● *The ancient past is exactly like our 1950s, and the distant future our 1960s.*

LUCKY (THE LUCKY CHARMS LEPRECHAUN)

Lucky the Leprechaun was "born" in 1964. His full name is L.C. Leprechaun, and according to him, his cereal is "Magically Delicious."

Although leprechauns are known for their distinctive feats of magic, Lucky's only power is that he can change ordinary, white marshmallows into miniscule geometric shapes with colors hardly ever found in nature.

The first magical marshmallow shapes were pink hearts, yellow moons, orange stars, and green clovers. Lucky Charms was the first cereal to include these marshmallow pieces, which are technically called "marbits." Marbits were invented by John Holahan, president of Post cereal, in 1963.

It has been said that leprechauns carry two leather pouches. In one there is a silver shilling— a magical coin that returns to his purse each time it is paid out; in the other, a gold coin to be used to bribe his way out of trouble. The gold coin usually turns to leaves or ashes once the leprechaun has parted with it. That being said, it stands to reason that no self-respecting leprechaun would ever think of sullying either of his pouches with marbits.

<u>What I Learned:</u>

  ● *More than even gold, Leprechauns need cereal.*

  ● *As it is with marshmallows, so it is with our souls.*

MAGILLA GORILLA

Magilla Gorilla was the star of "The Magilla Gorilla Show," which was produced by Hanna-Barbera between 1964 and 1967. Other characters included Punkin' Puss & Mushmouse, and Sheriff (ping-ping- ping) Ricochet Rabbit& Deputy Droop-a-Long (take-offs on Marshall Dillon and Chester from the TV show "Gunsmoke"). Like many Hanna-Barbera animals, Magilla sported snappy human accessories– specifically an undersized derby and a bow tie.

Magilla spent his days languishing in the front window of Mr. Peebles' pet shop, eating bananas and being a drain on the businessman's finances. Mr. Peebles would repeatedly mark down Magilla's price, but invariably, Magilla, was only purchased for a short time. The customers who bought Magilla, would inevitably return him, forcing Mr. Peebles to refund their money. Magilla ended most every episode with the chipper remark, "We'll try again next week."

The only customer who was truly interested in obtaining the trouble-prone ape for keeps was a little girl named Ogee ("Oh Gee!"), who lamentably never had enough money. During the cartoon's theme song, "We've Got a Gorilla for Sale," Ogee would always ask hopefully, "How much is that gorilla in the window?" a twist on the (then not-so) old standard, "How Much Is That Doggie in the Window?"

In Judaism, "the Magillah," is another name for the Book of Esther, which is read on Purim. Consequently, the term is also a colloquialism for a long, drawn-out story.

What I Learned:
- *Even though something's 1,000 lbs and could easily kill you, that doesn't mean it would make a bad pet.*
- *Everybody tough wears a derby.*
- *Gorillas are kinder and wiser than dyspeptic shopkeepers.*
- *Apes can roller-skate, although sooner or later, they'll crash.*

MIGHTY MOUSE

Mighty Mouse was originally created by Terrytoon cartoonist I. Klein as a super–powered housefly named "Superfly" (years before Curtis Mayfield), but studio head Paul Terry decided the character should be a mouse instead. An obvious imitation of Superman, he first appeared in 1942 in a theatrical short entitled "The Mouse of Tomorrow."

Mighty Mouse originally had a blue costume with a red cape like Superman; but over time this changed to a yellow costume with a red cape (probably to avoid a lawsuit). As with other Superman imitators, Mighty Mouse's superpowers allowed him to fly, and made him incredibly strong and invulnerable. In at least one cartoon he also had "X–ray vision."

The early, operatic Mighty Mouse cartoons often portrayed Mighty Mouse as ruthless. He would dole out a considerable amount of punishment, subduing the cats to the point of surrender. But that wasn't enough. Mighty Mouse would then chase down the fleeing felines and continue to beat them mercilessly, often grabbing them by the tails and hurling them to their doom. A favorite M.M. maneuver was to fly up just under a much larger opponent's chin and throw a blinding array of punches.

What I Learned:

● *Opera–singing mice can fly around and punch people.*

MR. MAGOO

Mister Magoo, a crotchety, nearsighted, old coot, first appeared in the 1949 UPA short "Ragtime Bear." Voiced by Jim Backus, Quincy Magoo was patterned after several real–life people. Backus claimed to have called upon observations of his father. Director John Hubley utilized his bullheaded uncle, and yet another probable source of inspiration was the persona of W. C. Fields. Mr. Magoo went on to star in a number of full–length classics, including "Mr. Magoo's Christmas Carol." In one of his many post–Warner's gigs, Mr. Magoo's tycoon uncle was voiced by Mel Blanc.

In 1957, the record album "Magoo in Hi–Fi" was released. Side 1 consisted of a dialog between Magoo and his nephew Waldo taking place while Magoo was attempting to set up his new sound system. Music on the album was composed and conducted by Dennis Farnon and his orchestra. Side 2, the Mother Magoo Suite, was a series of musical pieces which included two solos by Marni Nixon.

If, dear reader, you ever venture to my hometown of Brooklyn, NY, you will encounter many of Mr. Magoo's disciples blissfully motoring on our public streets.

What I Learned:
- *God protects innocents and fools.*
- *Blind faith is a powerful asset.*

◑ ***People will cheerfully ignore your odd and dangerous peccadilloes when you're rich.***

PEABODY'S IMPROBABLE HISTORY

Mr. Peabody, an extremely intelligent dog, and his adopted boy, Sherman (in a twist on the "boy and his dog" archetype), traveled through time to observe and assist the towering figures of history. Sherman's personality was that of an eager and energetic young puppy, Peabody's that of an uptight college professor. Both Mr. Peabody and Sherman wore black, oversized horn–rimmed glasses. The voices of Peabody and Sherman were provided by Bill Scott and Walter Tetley, respectively.

In the first episode, Mr. Peabody goes to court for the right to adopt Sherman. Successful, Peabody nonchalantly invents the WABAC machine (pronounced "Way Back") so Sherman can have "space to run." The WABAC machine is a name play on computers of the time, such as the UNIVAC and ENIAC.

At the end of every episode, Peabody and Sherman would talk to each other about what had just transpired, with Peabody always offering a bad pun related to the people or events being discussed. For example, when the Battle of Little Big Horn was completed, Peabody directed Sherman's attention to a hot dog vendor and remarked that this was the real "Custer's Last Stand."

Peabody and Sherman were characters on the Rocky and Bullwinkle show.

Legend holds that Peter Noone of the 60s British invasion band, Herman's Hermits, so named his group due to his resemblance to Sherman.

<u>*What I Learned:*</u>
- *Many run of the mill hounds can be insufferably pedantic. A few of them actually wear glasses.*
- *Even if a dog holds a PhD and joins Mensa, given the opportunity he will happily dig in the dirt.*

PEANUTS (CHARLIE BROWN)

Charles Schulz, America's most celebrated post World War II cartoonist, built an empire on the backs of midgets. In the late 1950s, Schulz made it chic and subversive for six-year olds to converse like jaded divorceés at a cocktail party.

In 1965, animator Bill Melendez brought good ol' Charlie Brown and his crew of sadistic tormentors to television. Backed by a great Vince Guaraldi tune (Linus and Lucy), our man Chuck assumed the mantle of leadership, managing his friends on a baseball team, sojourning out in the dead of winter to find the perfect Christmas tree, and generally trying to provide a conduit for the self–loathing which permeated his friends' miserable lives. Unfortunately, no matter what Charlie Brown did for these ungrateful ruffians, they would make sure to remind him that he was naught but a lonely and pathetic schmuck. Heavy is the head that wears the crown.

One can only surmise that if Charlie Brown were to somehow make it to adulthood, he would either become an SRO resident on disability, a depressive alcoholic who yells at strangers on the subway, or a Republican.

What I Learned:
- *The primary purpose of a leader is to give his followers someone to blame.*

PETER POTAMUS (AND SO–SO)

Peter Potamus and his Magic Flying Balloon, created by Hanna–Barbera during the early 1960s, featured Peter Potamus (the hippopotamus) and his sidekick, So–So the monkey. Peter was big, purple, and friendly, and was voiced by Daws Butler, imitating comedian Joe E. Brown. Episodes generally consisted of Peter and So–So exploring the world in his time–traveling hot air balloon, then somehow getting into trouble. When faced with certain doom, Peter used his "Hippo Hurricane Holler" to both vanquish his opponents and to blow So–So and himself to safety.

Peter Potamus and his Magic Flying Balloon debuted in 1964, as a syndicated series. It was divided into three segments: one of Peter Potamus, one of Breezly & Sneezly (a co–habiting polar bear and seal), and one of Yippee, Yappee & Yahooey (based on the Three Musketeers).

What I Learned:

- *If you're a big, fat blowhard in a pith helmet, travel through time with a monkey.*
- *Any decent hot air balloon can easily bridge the time–space continuum.*

POPEYE THE SAILOR (Max and Dave Fleischer)

Popeye the Sailor was created by cartoonist Elzie Segar, in his comic strip "Thimble Theatre." The strip originally had the characters of Olive Oyl, Ham Gravy (Olive's first boyfriend), Cole and Nana Oyl (Olive's parents) and Castor Oyl. On January 17, 1929, Popeye made his first appearance in the strip. His first words, a reply to the question, "Are you a sailor?" were "Ja think I'm a cowboy!" Needless to say, Popeye went on to be the most popular character in the strip and one of the greatest comic characters ever.

Thimble Theater was adapted into an animated cartoon series for Paramount Pictures by Fleischer Studios in 1933. Popeye made his film debut in "Popeye the Sailor," a 1933 Betty Boop cartoon (although Betty only made a brief appearance). "I Yam What I Yam" became the first entry in the regular Popeye the Sailor series.

The character of Popeye was originally voiced by William "Billy" Costello (Red Pepper Sam). When Costello's fame went to his head, he was replaced by former "in–between" animator Jack Mercer, beginning with "King of the Mardi Gras" in 1935. Olive Oyl was voiced by a number of actresses, but by far the most notable was Mae Questel, who also voiced Betty Boop. Various actors provided the voice of Bluto, including Gus Wickie, William Pennell, Jackson Beck, and Pinto Colvig (also the voice of "Goofy"). Other characters from the strip appeared briefly in the shorts, including Poopdeck Pappy, Eugene the Jeep, George W. Geezil, and the Goons.

Thanks to the series, Popeye became even more of a sensation. During the mid–1930s, polls taken by theater owners proved Popeye more popular than Mickey Mouse. In 1935, Paramount added to Popeye's popularity by sponsoring the "Popeye Club" as part of their Saturday matinee program. Popeye cartoons, including "Let's Sing with Popeye" were a regular part of the weekly meetings. For a 10 cent membership fee, club members were given a Popeye Kazoo, a membership card, the chance to become elected as the Club's "Popeye" or "Olive Oyl" and opportunities to win other valuable gifts.

The Popeye series was notable for its urban feel (the Fleischers operated out of New York City), its manageable variations on a simple theme (Popeye loses Olive to bully Bluto and must eat his spinach to defeat him), and the characters' "under–the–breath" mutterings (which began as ad–libs by

Mercer, who muttered so that his additions would not alter the timing of the completed animation).

Fleischer Studios produced 108 Popeye cartoons; 105 of them in black and white. The remaining three were two–reel (double–length) Technicolor specials billed as "Popeye Color Features": "Popeye the Sailor Meets Sindbad the Sailor," "Popeye the Sailor Meets Ali Baba's Forty Thieves," and "Aladdin and His Wonderful Lamp."

In 1941, with World War II becoming more of a source of concern in America, Popeye was enlisted into the U.S. Navy, as depicted in the 1941 short "The Mighty Navy." His costume was changed from the black shirt and white neckerchief to an official white Navy suit, and Popeye continued to wear the Navy suit in animated cartoons until the 1960s. Popeye periodically wore his original costume when at home on shore leave, as in the 1942 entry "Pip–Eye, Pup–Eye, Poop–Eye, An' Peep–Eye," which introduced his four identical nephews.

In July 2007, Paramount, Warner's and King Features finally resolved their decades–long licensing disputes, such that these national treasures were remastered and at long last made available on DVD!

What I Learned:
- *Give everyone a fair chance, but if they don't treat you right, sock 'em.*
- *Beauty is in the eye of the beholder.*

- *Spinach will make you stronger than a hamburger (although a hamburger is not very strong).*

- *I yam wot I yam, an' that's all wot I yam.*

- *An ordinary pipe can be used for many other things; (for example, an acetylene torch, a snorkel or a propeller...). You can also eat spinach through a pipe.*

- *It's a great mystery (or should I say, "myskery") where babies come from.*

POPEYE THE SAILOR *(Famous Studios)*

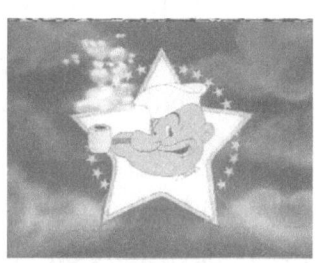

Fleischer Studios was dissolved in January 1942 when Max and Dave were both forced to resign from their company, ostensibly over losses from their groundbreaking "Superman" series. Paramount purchased the studio and renamed it Famous Studios. Appointing Seymour Kneitel and Isadore Sparber as its heads, production was continued on the shorts. Early Famous–era shorts were often World War II propaganda, featuring Popeye fighting Nazis and stereotyped Japanese soldiers.

In late 1943, the Popeye series went all–Technicolor, beginning with "Her Honor the Mare." Paramount moved the studio back to New York, and Mae Questel resumed voicing Olive Oyl. Jack Mercer, however, was drafted into the Navy. While he was unavailable, Mae Questel did double-duty as the voice of Popeye.

"Et tu, Brute?" For decades, Popeye fans have wondered wherefore Popeye's arch-enemy suffered his ignoble name change (from Bluto to Brutus). When King Features purchased Popeye from Paramount in 1957, Bluto's name was changed to Brutus because it was (wrongly) believed that Paramount Pictures (and their subsidiaries Fleischer Studios and Famous Studios) owned the rights to the name. Ironically, King Features owned the name all along as Bluto had been originally created for the comic strip. However, due to poor research, they failed to realize this and dubbed him Brutus to avoid copyright problems. "Brutus" appears in the 1960–1962 Popeye television cartoons (with his physical appearance changed, making him obese rather than muscular), but he is again "Bluto" (and back to his original muscular physique) in the 1978 Hanna-Barbera Popeye series and the 1980 live-action Popeye movie, as well as the 1987 Popeye and Son series also by Hanna-Barbera. The character was named Bluto in the 2004 movie Popeye's Voyage: The Quest for Pappy (with Popeye voiced brilliantly by Billy West).

Bobby London, who did the Popeye daily strip for six years, wrote and illustrated the "Return of Bluto" story where the 1932 version of Bluto returns and discovers a number of fat, bearded bullies have taken his place, calling themselves "Brutus" (each one being a different version of Popeye's rival).

What I Learned:
- *Random violence will sometimes get you what you want.*

- *If you're running late and discover a hole in your sock, tie a knot in it.*
- *If your head gets stuck in a pitcher, and the pitcher comes off, your head will retain that shape.*
- *It's just as great a myskery about nephews.*

QUICK DRAW MCGRAW

Quick Draw McGraw was the star of "The Quick Draw McGraw Show," Hanna–Barbera's third show (after Ruff & Reddy and The Huckleberry Hound Show). The show debuted in 1959; Quick Draw was voiced by actor Daws Butler.

Quick Draw (who was a horse) worked as a sheriff in the Old West. He was accompanied by his deputy, a Mexican burro named Baba Looey.

Quick Draw was well–intentioned, but dim. Usually, Baba Looey would make a more accurate assessment of the problem at hand. In his thick Mexican accent, Baba Looey would begin to advise Quick Draw: "Qeeks Draw, I theen..." whereupon Quick Draw would interrupt with his catchphrase: "Now hoooooold on thar, Baba Looey! I'll do the "thinnin' around here, and doooon't you forget it!"

Although Quick Draw was a horse who walked on two legs like a human (as did Baba Looey), this did not stop the show from depicting him riding into town on a realistic horse himself.

In a number of episodes, Quick Draw also assumed the identity of the masked vigilante, "El Kabong" (a parody of Zorro). As **El Kabong**, Quick Draw would attack his foes by swooping in on a rope and hitting them on the head with his guitar,(which he referred to as a "kabonger"), producing a distinctive "kabong" sound and destroying the guitar in the process. The "kabong" sound was created by a foley artist (the person who creates the sound effects for film) striking the detuned open strings of an acoustic guitar.

On the Howard Stern radio show, Gary Dell'Abate, who previously had been tormented with the moniker, "Boy Gary" (in reference to "Boy George"), acquired the nickname "Baba Booey" after mispronouncing the name of Quick Draw's sidekick while discussing his collection of animation art.

Quick Draw McGraw's supporting characters in The Quick Draw McGraw Show's two other segments were Augie Doggie and Doggie Daddy, a father–and–son pair of dogs (the father a Jimmy Durante parody), and Snooper and Blabber, a pair of detectives who were a cat and a mouse

What I Learned:

- *If somebody else on your team has a good idea, let them do "the thinnin'" for a change.*
- *There is a little known martial art centered around striking your opponent with a guitar.*

QUISP and QUAKE

Quisp and Quake were two sugar–sweetened breakfast cereals released in 1966 by The Quaker Oats Company and generally advertised together (during the same commercial) under the ruse of being competing products. The ads were created by Jay Ward of Rocky and Bullwinkle fame, and they used many of the same voices, including Daws Butler as the voice of Quisp (an alien) and William Conrad as the voice of Quake (a miner). The characters' conflict mirrored the struggle between hippies and conservatives.

What I Learned:
> *The great culture wars of the 1960s were all about cereal.*

THE ROAD RUNNER AND COYOTE

Wile E. Coyote (also known simply as "The Coyote") and **the Road Runner** were created by Chuck Jones in 1948 for Warner Brothers. Chuck Jones claimed to have gotten the idea for the characters from a Mark Twain book called "Roughing It," in which Twain noted that coyotes are starving and would chase a roadrunner.

Chuck Jones once said of his two most famous protagonists that "Wile E. is my reality, and Bugs Bunny is my goal." He originally created the Road Runner cartoons as a variation on traditional "cat and mouse" cartoons (such as Tom and Jerry) which were increasingly popular at the time. The major difference is that the audience's sympathy is drawn to the coyote, whose hunts always end in disaster. The cartoons' Southwestern setting also pays homage to the backgrounds of the Krazy Kat comic strip, by George Herriman.

What I Learned:

- *Don't keep doing the same thing expecting different results.*
- *Never buy goods from a company named Acme.*
- *The laws of physics can change. Our tangible world is illusory and in constant flux. Gravity cannot affect you unless you acknowledge its power. There's always time enough to scurry back to safety.*
- *We create our physical world. It's totally possible to paint a stretch of highway on a rock and run off into it.*

ROCKY AND BULLWINKLE

The heroes of this show were **Rocket "Rocky" J. Squirrel**, a flying squirrel (voiced by the great June Foray), and his best friend **Bullwinkle J. Moose** (voiced by Bill Scott), a dim-witted but good natured moose, who lived in the fictional town of Frostbite Falls, Minnesota (inspired by International Falls, Minnesota).

Each show included two "Rocky & Bullwinkle "shorts, which featured cliffhangers in the style of early movie serials. The shorts formed a storyline which crossed episode boundaries: the first and longest such story arc was "Jet Fuel Formula," which consisted of 40 shorts spanning twenty programs.

Each arc involved the moose and squirrel in adventures that took them all over the world, ranging from trying to find a missing ingredient for a rocket fuel formula, to searching for the monstrous whale "Maybe Dick," to preventing mechanical metal-munching moon mice from devouring the nation's television antennas.

In nearly every episode, the villains behind these schemes were the fiendish but inept agents of the fictitious nation of Pottsylvania, Boris Badenov (a pun on Boris Godunov) and Natasha Fatale (whose last name was a pun on the phrase "femme fatale"). Also trying to thwart our heros' plans were the evil "Mr. Big" and the sinister "Fearless Leader." Boris and Natasha are also the names of a young couple in Tolstoy's "War and Peace."

Rocky and Bullwinkle also marks the beginning of the letter "J" becoming a funny middle initial for a cartoon (e.g.: Homer J. Simpson). The letter was chosen for obvious reasons by Rocky's originator, Jay Ward.

Other segments on the show included "Fractured Fairy Tales," "Peabody and Sherman," "Dudley Do–Right," and "Aesop& Son" (which was narrated by Edward Everett Horton).

At the end of most episodes, the show's narrator, William Conrad, announced two possible titles for the next episode–the second title always a pun that was related to the first. For example, the narrator once intoned during an adventure taking place in a mountain range: "Be with us next time for "Avalanche Is Better than None," or "Snow's Your Old Man." And in a different episode: "Be with us next time for "50 cents lost" or "Get that halfback." Another episode said: "Be with us next time for "Bullwinkle buys a taco stand" or "Chilly today, hot tamale."

What I Learned:

- *Flounders write fan–mail.*

- *Angry lions can pop out of top hats*

- *Our life stories are narrated. Every so often we can stop everything and debate with the author.*

- *Even malevolent foreign spies are compelled by the need to join unions.*

SECRET SQUIRELL

Secret Squirrel was created by Hanna–Barbera, and voiced by the great Mel Blanc. Beginning as a costar on The Atom Ant/Secret Squirrel Show, which debuted in

1965, he was given his own show in 1966, but was reunited with Atom Ant for one more season in 1967.

Secret Squirrel capitalized on the extremely–popular spy genre of the mid–1960s (James Bond, Man from Uncle, Our Man Flint, etc.). Since Bond had a special, secret code number (007), Secret Squirrel had a number as well,("Agent 000"). While Bond took orders from "M," Secret's superior was "Double–Q." Secret was assisted in his adventures by a fez– wearing side–kick named Morocco Mole, patterned after Peter Lorre's character Ugarte in Casablanca. Morocco was voiced by Paul Frees.

The pair fought enemy agents with a variety of gadgets, including a machine gun cane, a collection of weapons kept inside Secret's coat, and various spy devices concealed in Secret's hat (which he almost never removed). Like Bond, who matched wits with a villain named, "Goldfinger", Secret Squirrel's arch enemy was known as "The Yellow Pinkie."

What I Learned:
- *The best secret agents are squirrels, because they're experts at guarding their nuts.*

SCOOBY–DOO

Scooby–Doo, Where are You! was the first incarnation of the long–running Hanna–Barbera Saturday morning cartoon

Scooby–Doo. It premiered in September 1969 and ran for two seasons on CBS. Twenty–five episodes were ultimately produced (seventeen in 1969–1970 and eight more in 1970–1971).

"Scooby–Doo, Where are You!" was the result of CBS and Hanna–Barbera's plans to create a non–violent Saturday morning program which would appease the parent watch groups that had protested the superhero–based programs of the 1960s. Originally titled "Mysteries Five," and later "Who's S–S–Scared?," "Scooby–Doo, Where are You!" underwent a number of changes from script to screen (the most notable of which was the removal of a musical group angle borrowed from "The Archie Show"). However, the basic concept–four teenagers (Fred, Daphne, Velma, and Shaggy) and a large goofy dog (Scooby–Doo) solving supernatural–related mysteries–was always in place.

The basic formula was this:

- The gang shows up in the Mystery Machine, en route to, or returning from, some "normal" teenage function.
- Their destination is suffering from a "ghost" or "monster."
- The kids volunteer to investigate the case.
- The gang splits up to cover more ground, with Fred and Velma finding clues, Daphne finding danger, and Shaggy and Scooby finding food, fun, and the ghost/monster, who starts to chase them.
- Eventually, enough clues are found to convince the gang that the ghost/monster is a fake, and a trap is set to capture it.
- The trap fails.
- Scooby Doo slips, and hurtles toward the ghost/monster, who falls down.

- The ghost/monster is apprehended and unmasked.
- The person in the ghost or monster suit turns out to be an angry but benign authority figure who is using the disguise to cover up criminal activity.
- The offender(s)–after giving the parting shot of "And I would have gotten away with it if it weren't for you meddling kids, and your dog!"–is then taken away to jail, and the gang continues on their way.

What I Learned:

- *Even if something seems really scary now, rest assured that it will eventually be unmasked as harmless, and things will work out just fine. In fact, that horrible monster you were so afraid of will probably wind up to be some lonely and scared person who's running from real or imagined monsters of their own.*

- *Take care of your buddy. If you've got a best pal, look out for them.*

- *Don't Bogart those snacks, my friend.*

THE SMURFS

In 1965, a black–and–white 90–minute animated film was made about **The Smurfs**, "Les Aventures des Schtroumpfs." It consisted of seven short cartoons made for Walloon TV and had a limited theatrical run in Belgium.

In 1976, Stuart R. Ross, an American media and entertainment entrepreneur who saw the Smurfs while traveling in Belgium, entered into an agreement with Editions

Dupuis and Peyo, acquiring North American rights to the characters. Subsequently, Ross launched the Smurfs in the United States in association with a California company, Wallace Berrie and Co., whose figurines, dolls and other Smurf merchandise became a huge success. NBC television executive Fred Silverman's daughter had a Smurf doll of her own and Silverman thought that a series based on the Smurfs might make a good addition to his Saturday–morning lineup.

The Smurfs secured their place in North American pop culture in 1980, when the Saturday–morning cartoon, "The Smurfs," produced by Hanna–Barbera Productions, debuted on NBC. The show became a major success for NBC, spawning spin–off television specials on an almost yearly basis. The Smurfs was nominated multiple times for Daytime Emmy awards, and won Outstanding Children's Entertainment Series in 1982–1983. The Smurfs television show enjoyed continued success until 1990, when, after a decade of success, NBC cancelled it due to decreasing ratings.

<u>*What I Learned:*</u>

- *Somehow, an entire society can thrive and prosper with only one woman.*
- *The big people are indeed out to get us.*
- *Never, ever, ever mow the lawn.*

SNAP, CRACKLE, POP

Third cousins by marriage to the Keebler elves, **Snap, Crackle and Pop**, reside in every single bowl of rice crispies, endowing this cereal with its constant cacophonous crunch. Tragically, these malevolent gamines are wholly responsible for millions of innocent children each year winding up with an earful of milk.

What I Learned:
◑ *Discover your talents and exploit them. If you're part of a cereal based rhythm group, be the best that you can be.*

SNUFFY SMITH

"Barney Google and **Snuffy Smith**" is one of the longest–running comic strips in history. Created in 1919, it first appeared in the sports section of the Chicago Herald and Examiner as "Take Barney Google, F'rinstance." It starred the cigar–smoking, sports–loving, poker–playing, girl–chasing, ne'er–do–well Barney Google. By October of that year, the strip was distributed by King Features to newspapers all across the country.

Barney's friend, Snuffy Smith is a stereotypical hillbilly. He lives in a shack, makes moonshine, is in constant trouble with the sheriff, and strives to never work. Occasionally, he steals chickens. In 1963, King Features put Snuffy into a cartoon trilogy, along with Beetle Bailey and Krazy Kat.

What I Learned:
- *Get drunk, steal chickens, and holler at your family. Therein lies the road to nirvana.*

SPEED RACER

Speed Racer began in Japan as the manga and anime series "Mach Go Go Go" from the anime studio Tatsunoko Productions.

Mach Go Go Go was first created by anime pioneer Tatsuo Yoshida as a manga series in the 1960s and made the jump to TV as an anime series in 1967. The central character was a young race car driver named Gō Mifune. Yoshida selected the names and symbolisms in his creation very carefully. The M logo on the hood of his race car and the front of his helmet stood for his family name Mifune, an homage to Japanese film star Toshiro Mifune (and not "Mach 5" as the English translation would suggest). His given name Gō is also a Japanese homonym for the number 5 (the number on his race car). This is also represented by the letter G embroidered on his shirt. The names themselves constitute a multi–lingual wordplay of the kind that started to become popular in Japanese culture at the time.

The English rights to Mach Go Go Go were acquired by American syndicate Trans–Lux. The main character Go Mifune was given the name **"Speed Racer"** in the English version. A major editing and dubbing effort was undertaken by producer Peter Fernandez, who also voiced many of the characters, including Speed Racer himself. Fernandez was also responsible for a retooling of the theme song's melody and its subsequent English lyrics. When the series emerged before U.S. TV audiences as Speed Racer, fans were quickly drawn to its sophisticated plots involving fiendish conspiracies, violent action, hard–driving racing, and soulful characters with sparkling eyes. In an effort to squeeze the complicated plotlines into existing lip movements, the frenetic pace of the dubbing made Speed Racer famous for its quirky "fast" dialogue.

"The Mach Five" is a technological marvel containing a plethora of high–tech gadgets. These gadgets were easily deployed by pressing buttons marked 'A' through 'G' on the steering wheel hub. The "chyock chyock" sound effect played whenever the car jumped through the air is instantly recognizable to the show's fans.

The Buttons had the following functions:

- Button A: "Releases powerful jacks to boost the car so anyone can quickly make any necessary repairs or adjustments." Although designed for this function, the auto jacks can also be used to "jump" the car short distances at high speeds.
- Button B: Toggles special grip tires for traction over rough terrain (firm, icy, or unsteady ground, ocean floor, vertical mountainsides). At the same time, 5,000 horsepower is distributed equally to each wheel by auxiliary engines.

- Button C: For use traveling over heavily wooded terrain. A matched pair of powerful rotary saws protrudes from the front of the Mach 5 to cut away many obstacles.
- Button D: Releases a powerful transparent cover which seals the cockpit into an air–tight chamber. The cover is bullet and crash–proof. The cockpit becomes a water–tight chamber which then allows the car to be completely submerged under water.
- Button E: Controls special illumination lights "which can be controlled singularly or in tandem," and which allows the driver to see more clearly than with ordinary headlights. When used with the "night shades" attached to Speed's helmet, his vision is enhanced with infrared light.
- Button E was later modified to activate mini–wings that would slide out from under the car to assist Speed in long jumps.
- Button F: Used when the Mach Five is submerged. An oxygen canister supplies the cockpit with breathable air. A periscope can then be raised to scan the surface of the water. Everything that is viewed through a relay to a video screen. The 100–pound auxiliary supply of oxygen is enough to last for thirty minutes.
- Button G: Releases a homing robot from under the hood of the car. The homing robot can carry pictures or tape recorded messages to an intended party. The robot also can carry handwritten messages, X–ray film, and other types of code. It has been used as a means of self–defense by flying at adversaries. The bird–like device is operated by a built–in remote control within the cockpit. A separate button sends the robot "home."

What I Learned:

- *You've an excellent chance to score with the ladies when you're a handsome and dashing young race–car driver, but what really drives the chicks crazy is a monkey!*

- *It might not be the best idea to store the only copy of your secret blueprints in the windshield of a race–car.*

SPIDER MAN

Spider Man (a.k.a. Peter Benjamin Parker) was the son of Richard and Mary Parker, who worked as S.H.I.E.L.D. agents, and who were killed on a mission involving the Red Skull. The infant Peter Parker was left in the care of his Uncle Ben and Aunt May Parker, who had a modest home in the Forest Hills section of Queens, New York (these days, not so modest). The aging couple loved Peter, but he was a somewhat unpopular young fellow, due to his being a wuss. Over time, he developed into a lonely, timid, yet exceptionally bright teenager who showed more interest in his studies (especially science) than in any kind of social life.

One fateful day, Peter Parker attended a science exhibition where he was bitten by a radioactive spider. The bite gave Peter an array of spider–like powers, including wall–crawling, superhuman strength/agility, and an extra–sensory "spider–sense." Rarely mentioned, the spider bite also accelerated Peter's latent predilection to be a wiseass. Naturally, being an underprivileged NY orphan, Peter set out to use his new powers to get rich, and, as everyone knows, the surest way to fame and fortune is professional wrestling. After quickly becoming a celebrity, Peter appeared on a television special, but afterward allowed a thief to escape the TV station, asserting (in classis NY style), that it wasn't his problem. He came to regret his inaction when he found out that the very same burglar had killed his Uncle Ben. Realizing that he could have prevented his uncle's demise, the guilt–ridden Peter committed to a life of crime fighting, driven by his uncle's words, "With great power there must also come great responsibility."

This volatile mix of selfless obligation, guilt, all–purpose teenage angst, and New York wisenheimer, made up the psyche of Spider–Man.

What I Learned:

- **Bombastic newspaper editors can get away with wearing Hitler Moustaches.**

- **Sometimes the nerd comes out ahead, particularly if he can fly through the air and shoot webs and stuff.**

- **Little pumpkins will explode if you throw them.**

PRINCE NAMOR – THE SUBMARINER

One of a series of cartoons made by the "Merry Marvel Marching Society "(Marvel Comics) in 1966, **The Submariner** lived in the underwater city of Atlantis, and had a love/hate relationship with the surface dwellers. Prince Namur is one of the oldest superhero characters. He was created by writer–artist Bill Everett in Spring, 1939 for Funnies, Inc., one of the first "packagers" in the early days of comic books that would supply comics on demand to publishers looking to enter the new medium. Initially created for an unpublished promotional comic, the Sub–Mariner first appeared publicly in Marvel Comics #1 (Oct. 1939), the first comic book from Timely Comics, (the 1930s–1940s predecessor of Marvel Comics). During that period, known to historians and fans as the Golden Age of Comic Books, the Sub–Mariner was one of Tim Ely's top three characters, along with Captain America and the original Human Torch (years before the Fantastic Four).

The son of a human sea captain and a princess from Atlantis, Namur possessed the super–strength and aquatic abilities of the "Homo–Merman's" race. Throughout the years, he has alternately been a good–natured but short–fused superhero, and a hostile invader seeking vengeance for perceived wrongs that misguided surface–dwellers committed against his kingdom.

Other cartoons in the series included, "Captain America," "The Incredible Hulk," "The Invincible Iron Man," and "The Mighty Thor."

What I Learned:
- *The people who live underwater don't like us very much – and can you blame them?*
- *The lost continent of Atlantis was originally populated by Vulcan's.*

TENNESEE TUXEDO

Tennessee Tuxedo was introduced on CBS in response to the famed 1961 speech by FCC Chairman Newton R. Minow, in which he referred to television as a "vast wasteland." Tennessee, voiced by comedian Don Adams (who portrayed Maxwell Smart on Get Smart, and later voiced Inspector Gadget), educated as well as entertained us.

Tennessee, a wise–cracking penguin, and his dim–witted pal, Chumley (voiced by Bradley Bolke), resided in the Megalopolis Zoo. They were constantly scheming against zookeeper Stanley Livingston (voiced by Mort Marshall) and his assistant Flunky (voiced by Kenny Delmar), in an attempt to raise the quality of zoo–life. Their projects always required the assistance of their educated friend, Phineas J. Whoopee (voiced by Larry Storch), and his 3–D BB (a three dimensional blackboard). The 3–D BB helped demonstrate basic scientific principles through the use of instructional film clips.

The series initially included repeat episodes of "The Hunter" and "Tooter Turtle" from "King Leonardo". These segments were later replaced by newer components, including "The World of Commander McBragg" and "Klondike Kat".

What I Learned:
- *An incredible amount of worthless junk can be stuffed into a closet.*
- *Zoo animals are both thoughtful and reasonable, and many of them dream of being people.*

THE MIGHTY THOR

One of a series of cartoons made by the "Merry Marvel Marching Society" (Marvel Comics) in 1966, **The Mighty Thor** is the Norse God of thunder, who decided to come to earth and fight crime. He masquerades as a self-effacing disabled man with a walking stick. When he strikes the walking stick on the ground, it becomes his magical hammer, thus transforming him into the Mighty Thor.

Actually, the coming to earth part, his father decided for him. Thor's father, Odin determined that his son needed to lacked humility so he placed him (without memories of godhood) into the body and memories of a disabled human medical student, Donald Blake. While on vacation in Norway, Blake discovered Thor's (his) disguised hammer Mjolnir, and striking it against a rock, transformed.

Also featured in the show were Thor's dad Odin (Asgaard's Capo di tutti Capo) and Thor's evil brother Loki (God of mischief).

Other cartoons in the series included, "Captain America," "The Incredible Hulk," "Submariner", and "The Invincible Iron Man."

In 1969, my older sister threw a hammer at me in a fight. It's true – cartoons do promote violence.

What I Learned:

- *The only thing immortal Gods are really interested in is fighting crime.*
- *When they've got you cornered, throw a hammer.*

TOM TERRIFIC

Created by Gene Deitch of Terrytoons (which had recently been purchased by CBS, the network that broadcast Captain Kangaroo), **Tom Terrific** ran in a series of five-minute cartoons created specifically for the Captain Kangaroo show from 1957-1959, and was rerun on Kangaroo for years thereafter. For several years after 1962, Tom Terrific would be broadcast every other week, alternating with Lariat Sam, another Terrytoons creation.

Drawn in a simple style, it featured a boy hero, Tom Terrific, who lived in a tree house and could transform himself into anything he liked thanks to his magic "thinking cap" funnel hat, which also enhanced his intelligence. He had a sidekick, Mighty Manfred the Wonder Dog, and an arch-foe named Crabby Appleton, whose motto was "Rotten to the core!" Other foes included Mr. Instant, the Instant Thing King; Captain Kidney Bean; Sweet Tooth Sam, the Candy Bandit; and Isotope Feaney. All the voices were done by Lionel Wilson.

What I Learned:

- *With a little bit of spunk, and a free imagination, I can be anything.*
- *Wearing a tin-foil pyramid on my head will indeed make me smarter.*

TOP CAT

Top Cat, called T.C. by close friends, is the leader of a gang of Runyonesque New York alley cats: "Fancy Fancy", "Spook," "Benny the Ball", "The Brain," and "Choo Choo". Top Cat and his gang were inspired by characters from the "The Phil Silvers Show," (a.k.a., "You'll never be rich"). Maurice Gosfield, who played Private Duane Doberman on The Phil Silvers Show, also provided the voice for Benny the Ball in Top Cat (Benny's rotund appearance was based on Gosfield too). Arnold Stang's voicing of Top Cat strongly resembled Phil Silvers.

A frequent plotline revolved around the local policeman, Officer Dibble, and his ineffective attempts to evict the gang from the city. Dibble's appearance was modeled on Allen Jenkins who did his voice. A "Dibble" is a pointed gardening tool, used to plant seeds.

What I Learned:

- *With a slippery wit and a team of flunkies, you can usually hustle the world.*

❧ One man's garbage is another man's treasure. This may or may not apply literally to food.

TOUCAN SAM

Fruit Loop's mascot is **Toucan Sam**, a blue cartoon toucan with a striped beak. Although his beak originally had two pink stripes, during the 1970s it became a tradition that each stripe on his beak represented one of the flavors of the cereal. (red = cherry, yellow = lemon, orange = orange). The additions of new flavors have made this color scheme no longer accurate. There are now, in fact, seven different flavors in the cereal.

Toucan Sam was originally voiced by Mel Blanc, using a standard American accent. The ad agency later decided to switch to the English accent more commonly associated with the character. They then employed Paul Frees to do what is, in effect, an imitation of Ronald Coleman (the same voice he used as "Ape" on "George of the Jungle"). In the most recent cartoon advertisements for Froot Loops, Toucan Sam's voice has been performed by Canadian voice actor Maurice LaMarche.

Zoologically speaking, Toucan Sam is a Keel–billed Toucan, known in Latin as "Ramphastos sulfuratus."

What I Learned:

❧ Follow your nose. Anything worthwhile should pass the "smell test."

- *If you have a humungous honker, embrace it. Use it to sniff out snack foods.*

THE TRIX RABBIT

Trix cereal was first marketed in 1954. The original character on the Trix box from 1954 to 1959 was a stick figure flamingo. In August 1959, on a request from the supervisor of General Mills' ad agency, Joe Harris created the rabbit. The rabbit (voiced by Delo States and later Russell Horton) kept trying to trick kids into giving him a bowl of Trix cereal. Unfortunately for him, the children were too smart. Ultimately, when they felt that the rabbit's frustration had reached its zenith, the malicious brats would taunt him with, "Silly rabbit, Trix are for kids," leaving him "high and dry" as they skipped gleefully into the sunset.

Much like Warner Brothers' Wile E. Coyote, the Trix Rabbit's constant struggle to obtain the unobtainable elicited sympathy from his viewers.

What I Learned:
- *Practice detachment when striving for your goals. Desperation will repel that which you seek.*
- *Sugar-crazed children are sadists.*

UNDERDOG

Underdog was yet another burlesque of (or homage to) Superman. The premise was that "humble and lovable" Shoeshine Boy, a nebbish dog, was in "real life" the superhero Underdog. George Irving narrated, and Wally Cox provided the voices of both Underdog and Shoeshine Boy. When villains threatened, Shoeshine Boy ducked into a telephone booth where he transformed into the caped and costumed hero, invariably destroying the booth in the process.

Underdog almost always spoke in rhyme. For example:

"When Polly's in trouble, I am not slow, It's hip! hip! hip! and away I go." and

"There's no need to fear, Underdog is here."

The villains always managed to menace Sweet Polly Purebred (voiced by Norma McMillan), a platinum blonde canine TV reporter (reminiscent of Lois Lane), as part of their nefarious schemes. When in trouble she would sing, "Oh where, oh where has my Underdog gone?"

Villains included Simon Bar Sinister, a mad scientist with a voice reminiscent of Lionel Barrymore, and Riff Raff, a wolf gangster based on actor George Raft. Other villains included "The Electric Eel," "Battyman," and "Overcat." In medieval heraldry, a "Bar Sinister" indicates a person who was born out of wedlock, or "a bastard."

When Underdog's power waned, he would take drugs– chanting, "The secret compartment of my ring I fill, with an Underdog Super Energy Pill."

What I Learned:

- *It scares the hell out of people if you recite some sort of sing–song rhyme just before you hit them, (e.g., "to break up this ruckus, I'll pummel your tuchus").*
- *Any U.S. coin will bend if you grip it between your teeth.*
- *Even rhyming superhero dogs have a soft spot for platinum blondes.*

WALLY GATOR

By 1963, Hanna Barbera had begun to run out of prime–time sitcoms to copy, so they started copying themselves. **Wally Gator** (voiced by Daws Butler), lived in a national park, spent his days trying to get around the authority of the park ranger and conspired to steal pic–a– nic baskets. Ok. I added the last one. Somehow it all seemed very familiar. Now where have we seen this before... hmmm. Was he smarter than the average gator??

Other segments on this show were "Lippy the Lion and his sidekick Hardy Har Har" and "Touché Turtle and his sidekick "Dum Dum."

What I Learned:

 ● *Wild alligators are sort of friendly, and fun to pal around with – just like wild bears.*

WINKY–DINK AND YOU

Winky–Dink and You was a CBS show that aired from 1953 to 1957, and again in syndication from 1969 to 1973. It was hosted by Jack Barry, and featured the exploits of Winky–Dink (voiced by the great Mae Questel), and his dog Woofer.

Hailed by Bill Gates as "the first interactive TV show," the show's central gimmick was the use of a "magic drawing screen," which was essentially a large piece of plastic that stuck to the television screen via static electricity. A kit containing the screen and various crayons could be purchased through the mail for 50 cents. At a climactic scene in every cartoon, Winky–Dink would wind up in a perilous scene which contained a connect–the–dot picture. He would then prompt the children at home to complete the picture, and the finished result would help him continue the story. Some examples include drawing a bridge to cross a river, or a cage to trap a dangerous lion.

Quite a few children would omit the Magic Screen and draw on the television screen itself, to the consternation of their parents. Mea Culpa!

The show was wildly successful due to this pioneering interactive marketing scheme, and Winky-Dink was one of television's most popular characters during the 1950s. The show was revived again in syndication for 65 episodes beginning in 1969 and ending in 1973. However, the show's production was halted despite its modest popularity due to concerns about radiation in television sets affecting children and because of parental complaints about children drawing on the TV.

What I Learned:

- *Don't sit that close to the TV. You'll hurt your eyes.*
- *Don't draw on the TV. You'll hurt your ass (when you get spanked).*

YOGI BEAR AND BOO-BOO

Yogi Bear made his debut in 1958 as a supporting character on The Huckleberry Hound Show. He became very popular, and in 1961 was given his own show, which also included the segments "Snagglepuss" and "Yakky Doodle." There was even a feature film, "Hey There, It's Yogi Bear!" in 1964. Over the years he appeared in many other spin-off series as well, including "Yogi's Gang" (1973), "Yogi's Space Race" (1978), "Galaxy Goof-Ups" (1978), "Yogi's Treasure Hunt" (1985), "The New Yogi Bear Show" (1988) and "Yo Yogi" (1991).

Like many Hanna–Barbera characters, Yogi's personality and mannerisms were based on a popular celebrity of the time, specifically Art Carney's character Ed Norton, from "The Honeymooners." Yogi's name is a nod to famed Yankee catcher "Yogi Berra."

The plot of most Yogi cartoons centered around his antics in Jelly stone Park, (a spoof of Yellowstone National Park). Yogi, accompanied by his best pal and devoted conscience, Boo–Boo, would attempt to steal picnic baskets from park campers, much to the dismay of Park Ranger Smith.

What I Learned:

- *Sometimes, to get what you want, you need to break the rules.*
- *If you're going through life as a rule–breaker, find a good buddy with ethics. Rely upon that buddy to be your moral compass.*

LATTER DAY PROPHETS
(YUP, I STILL WATCH 'EM!)

FAIRLY ODD PARENTS

Setting: the fictional town of Dimmsdale (somewhere in California). Our hero: 10-year-old Timmy Turner.

An only child, Timmy is often left by his negligent parents in the care of evil babysitter, Vicky. In response to his grim situation, he is granted a pair of fairy godparents, named Cosmo and Wanda, who were charged by Fairyworld with making Timmy happy. Unfortunately, Cosmo is somewhat dumb, and Timmy's wishes often go awry. Wanda, Cosmo's more sensible wife must devote her time to ensuring both Timmy's and Cosmo's safety.

Since Cosmo and Wanda became Timmy's fairy godparents, a new host of characters entered his life: his maniacal fairy-obsessed teacher, Mr. Crocker and various magical creatures such as Mama Cosma (Cosmo's mother), Jorgen Von Strangle (the commandant of fairy world), Norm the Genie, and The Pixies (not the rock group).

Timmy's **Fairly Odd Parents** (a pun on "fairy godparents") are mindful of their secretive existence and disguise themselves as various animals and objects when in public. While disguised, they always have the same colors to identify each of them: Cosmo is always a light green, and Wanda is always a light pink. The only exception is that when they become goldfish; only their eyes retain their identifying colors. Other than Timmy, no one seems to notice green and pink talking birds, or notebooks with faces and gold crowns.

Most episodes end with a fairy based "deus ex machina." Many episodes are resolved by Timmy yelling, "I wish everything was back to normal!" or something similar, with the occasional tag line, ..."and no one remembered any of this."

What I Learned:

- *Our guardian angels take many forms. Don't be attached to appearance.*
- *Be very, very, careful what you wish for.*
- *In addition to being a movie star and the Governor of California, Arnold Schwarzenegger is also the military commander of all fairies.*

FOSTER'S HOME FOR IMAGINARY FRIENDS

In this world, **Imaginary Friends** become real the instant a child imagines them. Unfortunately for imaginary friends, children outgrow them. When that happens, imaginary friends are left to fend for themselves. Foster's Home for Imaginary Friends was founded by the elderly Madame Foster to provide a foster home (hence the title) for abandoned imaginary friends. Their motto is "Where good ideas are not forgotten." In the episode "Setting a

President," we are told that there are 1,340 imaginary friends in Foster's Home. However, in the episode "Emancipation Complication" Madame Foster states that there are in fact 2,037 Imaginary Friends. I would conclude therefore, that the population of imaginary friends is rising.

What I Learned:
- *What have all the self–help gurus been telling us? See it. Believe it. Claim it. This goes for imaginary friends as well.*
- *If someone is asking for chocolate milk they really want juice.*
- *Some bulls are friendly and speak Spanish.*

HOMER, MARGE AND THE KIDDIES

The Simpsons is an Emmy and Peabody Award–winning sitcom created by Matt Groening for the Fox Network. It's a satirical parody of the Middle American lifestyle epitomized by its titular family, which consists of Homer, Marge, Bart, Lisa, Maggie, Snowball II, and Santa's Little Helper. Set in the town of Springfield (somewhere in these United States – we're never told where), the show lampoons many aspects of the human condition, as well as American culture, society as a whole and even television itself. As of this writing, it is the longest–running sitcom in the U.S.

The family was conceived by Groening shortly before a pitch for a series of animated shorts with James L. Brooks. He sketched out his version of a dysfunctional family, and named the characters after members of his own family, choosing Bart for his own name. The shorts became a part of The Tracey Ullman Show on April 19, 1987. After a three–season run, the sketch was developed further into a half–hour prime time show on its own.

On January 14, 2000, the Simpsons was awarded a star on the Hollywood Walk of Fame.

In 2007, The Simpsons celebrated its 20th anniversary, and a feature–length film was released.

What I Learned:

- *Even an alcoholic, child–abusing, self–destructive moron can own a house.*
- *There is a perfect soul mate for everyone.*
- *Paul McCartney vacations on the roof of a Quick–E–Mart.*
- *Beyond the nexus of dream and imagination, exists a wonderful world of chocolate.*

POWERPUFF GIRLS

The Powerpuff Girls live in the fictional city of Townsville. They were created by Professor Utonium, who was attempting to create little girls (by combining sugar, spice, and everything nice), when he accidentally knocked a beaker of "Chemical X" into the mixture.

Blossom, has long red hair, pink eyes, and dresses in pink. She is the "commander and the leader," and is therefore the most mature, although her personality can spill over into being fussy, overbearing and analytical.

Bubbles, has blonde hair in pigtails, blue eyes, and dresses in blue. She is "the joy and the laughter," meaning that she's defined by her innocence, playfulness and gentle demeanor. She also has a tendency to be naive, submissive and overemotional, leading to her often being (unfairly) regarded, by friends and foes alike, as the group's weak link.

Buttercup, has short black hair, green eyes, and dresses in green. She is "the toughest fighter," in other words, she's the tomboy. She has a habit, though, of letting her aggression get the better of her, making her reckless, stubborn and overly-aggressive, and she can be said to possess a mean, vindictive streak not shared by her sisters.

The girls have many superpowers similar to, and in some cases surpassing Superman, including:

- Super–strength
- Flight
- Super–speed
- Ability to project a variety of energy blasts
- Limited invulnerability
- Ferocious Fiery Feline (the girls combine to create a cat of pure fire)
- Creating after–image doubles (who can also fight)
- Morphing into a ball

Major recurring villains include:

Mojo Jojo (voiced by Roger L. Jackson): A mad scientist chimp with vast intelligence, notable for his Japanese accent and convoluted manner of speaking.

Fuzzy Lumpkins (voiced by Jim Cummings): A large, husky, furry pink hillbilly monster who loves his hunting gun (or "boomstick") and his banjo (nicknamed "Joe"), and who will shoot anything he finds "on his property."

Him (Voiced by Tom Kane): A mysterious, super powerful, red–skinned, and effeminate devil–like creature with crab–like hands. He is so evil that his real name can never be said. He often disguises himself or creates psychological events or catastrophes which he uses as an attempt to cause the Powerpuff Girls to break mentally.

What I Learned:

- *Monkeys are evil and want to take over the world.*
- *Who needs fingers when you can fly?*

REN AND STIMPY

Ren Höek and Stimpson J. Cat, best pals and cartoon pioneers in the realm of same-sex marriage (in Puppet World, that honor, of course, goes to Bert and Ernie), were created by animator John Kricfalusi.

Ren Höek, a neurotic "asthma–hound" Chihuahua, and Stimpson J. Cat (a.k.a. Stimpy), a fat, red, feline simpleton, meander through life exploring the workaday world and all manner of disgusting bodily functions.

Produced by the children's cable network Nickelodeon, The Ren & Stimpy Show had a reputation for being subversive. At the time, its level of gross–out humor was matched only by such shows as Beavis and Butthead (on MTV). The show was canceled around 1996, shortly after the Nickelodeon's newer hit "the Rugrats" (which was far more wholesome) became popular.

What I Learned:

- *Stray socks travel to an entirely different planet.*
- *Within our belly–buttons is an incredible world ruled by a lint king.*
- *Burl Ives is frightening.*

SOUTHPARK

Set in a tiny village in Colorado, the adorable scamps of **South Park** cavort and frolic in their wholesome mountain town, in a spirit of understanding, tolerance and cooperation.

One recurring gag for the first few seasons was that Kenny, (who is burdened with an unfortunate speech impediment created by his coat's hood), would die in every episode only to return the following week. At his demise, one of his buddies (usually Stan), would yell, "Omigod! They killed Kenny!" To which Kyle would add, "You Bastards!" Eventually rats or buzzards would drag Kenny away.

Other whimsical characters included the overbearing, bigoted, and "big–boned" Eric Cartman," Kyle's mother, "Mrs. Broslovsky," "Chef" (played by the late Isaac Hayes), "Jesus Christ," "Santa Claus," and "Mr. Hanky" (who is a small, yet jovial turd).

What I Learned:
- *The most delectable kosher treat ever devised is Gafagahaga.*
- *A marvelous way to show that special someone that you care is to throw up on them.*

SPONGEBOB SQUAREPANTS

Sponge Bob Square Pants is a sponge who lives in a pineapple "under the sea." His octopus neighbor Squidward Q. Tentacles lives in a Moai head and sounds a lot like Jack Benny.

Sponge Bob's other neighbor and best friend (one house down from Squidward) is a pink sea star named Patrick, who lives under a rock. When Patrick and Sponge Bob have too much fun, Squidward gets annoyed.

Sponge Bob's house pet is a snail named Gary, whose "meow" is identical to a cat. In addition, underwater worms bark exactly like dogs, and are kept on chains.

Sponge Bob works at the Krusty Krab, a fast–food restaurant, as a fry cook alongside Squidward who is a cashier. The Krusty Krab is owned by Mr. Eugene H. Krabs, commonly referred to as "Mr. Krabs." Spongebob's job at the Krusty Krab is to make Krabby Patties.

Sheldon J. Plankton (commonly referred to as "Plankton") is Mr. Krabs' archrival who owns a less popular fast–food restaurant called The Chum Bucket across the street. Plankton spends most of his time plotting to steal the recipe for Krabby Patties.

Another of Sponge Bob's friends is Sandy Cheeks. Sandy is a squirrel who lives in an underwater dome. When not inside her tree–dome, she wears a diving suit with a globe helmet to protect her and allow her to keep breathing.

What I Learned:

- *When in doubt, pinky out.*

- *Sea–bears won't attack you if you're within the magic circle.*

- *You can sun–bathe, surf, go fishing, enjoy running water, and start a fire – all on the bottom of the ocean.*

- *Squirrels come from Texas, are stronger than lobsters and sharks and make excellent scientists.*

THE COMPANIES

DiC ENTERTAINMENT

DiC Entertainment, (pronounced "deek") was created in 1971 by Jean Chalopin in Luxembourg, as a subsidiary of Radio–Television Luxembourg (RTL). DiC stands for Diffusion, Information et Communication. The company's United States headquarters is in Burbank.

In addition to animated (and occasionally live–action) television shows, DiC has produced live–action feature films in collaboration with Disney, including 1998's "Meet the Deedles" and 1999's "Inspector Gadget".

DiC – Gurus and Philosophers

- Action Man
- The Adventures of Teddy Ruxpin
- Archibald le Magi–chien
- The Buzz on Maggie
- Captain Planet and the Planeteers
- Care Bears
- Dennis the Menace
- Gadget Boy & Heather
- Heathcliff
- Hulk Hogan's Rock 'n Wrestling
- Inspector Gadget
- The Legend of Zelda
- Liberty's Kids
- Mary–Kate And Ashley In Action
- New Kids On The Block
- Rainbow Brite
- Sailor Moon
- Sherlock Holmes in the 22nd Century
- Sonic Underground
- Strawberry Shortcake
- Street Sharks
- The Super Mario Bros. Super Show
- Swamp Thing
- The Real Ghostbusters
- Trollz (In association with DAM)
- Yin Yang Yo!
- Captain Planet
- The Smurfs
- Stargate Infinity
- Astroboy (1980 TV series)
- Bump in the Night

FAMOUS STUDIOS

Famous Studios was created by Paramount Pictures after they foreclosed on the Fleischers in 1942. Isadore Sparber, Dan Gordon, and Max Fleischer's son-in-law Seymour Kneitel became the new heads of the studio, which was moved from Miami back to New York.

Although the studio still carried much of the staff from the Fleischer regime, the quality of the output deteriorated. In general, Famous Studios raised the level of violence and lowered the level of whimsy.

FAMOUS STUDIOS – Gurus and Philosophers

(Carried over from the Fleischer period):
- Popeye the Sailor
- Superman
- Screen Songs (resurrected in 1947)

(Begun under the new management):
- Baby Huey
- Casper the Friendly Ghost
- Herman and Katnip
- Little Lulu(which was eventually replaced with an imitation called Little Audrey)

FILMATION

Filmation was founded in 1963 by radio announcer Norman Prescott, former Bozo the Clown animator Lou Scheimer and former Disney animator Hal Sutherland. They began by doing animated commercials and documentaries until 1965, when the company won a successful bid to produce Superman.

While many people fault Filmation's cost–cutting techniques, they have to admit that Filmation produced exciting, imaginative shows that are remembered fondly. Also worth noting, is that while almost all other animation series were being sent overseas, Filmation did all of their production in the States.

FILMATION – Gurus and Philosophers

- The New Adventures of Superman
- Aquaman/Superman Hour of Adventure
- The Archies
- Batman/Superman Hour
- Fantastic Voyage
- Archie's Comedy Hour
- The Hardy Boys
- Sabrina, the Teenage Witch
- Archie's Fun House
- Will the Real Jerry Lewis Please Sit Down?
- Sabrina and the Groovie Goolies
- Fat Albert and the Cosby Kids
- The Brady Kids
- Everything's Archie
- My Favorite Martians
- Lassie's Rescue Rangers
- Star Trek
- U.S. of Archie
- Shazam!
- Shazam–Isis Hour
- The Adventures of Waldo Kitty
- Tarzan, Lord of the Jungle
- The Batman–Tarzan Adventure Hour *(seems like almost too much adventure for one show, eh?)*
- The Bang Shang Lalapalooza Show
- The Superwitch Show
- The Fabulous Funnies
- The New Adventures of Flash Gordon
- Fat Albert and the Cosby Kids
- The New Adventures of Mighty Mouse
- Fat Albert Easter Special
- Jason, of Star Command (Live Action)
- A Snow White Christmas Special
- The New Adventures of Tom and Jerry
- Fat Albert "Follow the Leader"
- Fat Albert Department of Energy Spot
- Tarzan, Lone Ranger, Zorro Adventure Hour *(I stand corrected – see above.)*
- Blackstarr
- The Kid Super Power Hour
- Gilligan's Planet *(this is my favorite Filmation title of all. If castaways are funny on an island, they'll be hilarious in space. The sad thing is Filmation was able to get almost all of the original actors to voice it).*
- He–Man and the Masters of the Universe
- Ghost Busters

Everything I need to know, I learned from Cartoons!

FLEISCHER STUDIOS

Before Hanna–Barbera, before Warner Bros., before even Disney–there was Max Fleischer. The Fleischer Studios, located at 1600 Broadway, in New York City, were founded in 1921 by brothers Max and Dave Fleischer, who ran the company from its inception until they were fired by their parent company Paramount Pictures in 1942. In its prime, it was the most significant competitor to Walt Disney, and is notable for bringing to the screen Koko the Clown, Betty Boop, Popeye the Sailor, and Superman.

The company had its start when Max Fleischer invented a device called a rotoscope which produced extremely realistic animation by allowing artists to trace over live action film. Using this device, the Fleischer brothers got a contract with Bray Studios in 1919 to produce their own cartoon series called Out of the Inkwell, featuring their first character, Koko the Clown. This was very successful and gave them the confidence to start their own studio in 1921.

Throughout the 1920s, the studio was one of the top producers of animation, with clever humor and numerous innovations. These included Ko–Ko Song Cartunes, sing–along shorts (featuring "The Famous Bouncing Ball"), and extended length educational films such as "The Einstein Theory of Relativity."

The studio even produced some experimental sound films years before "The Jazz Singer," and more importantly, years before Disney's "Steamboat Willie." Their sound cartoons attracted little interest, because at the time, only a few theaters were equipped with electronic speakers.

With the full adoption of sound films in the late 1920s, the studio was one of the few animation companies to successfully make the transition with "Screen Songs," a continuation of the earlier "Ko–Ko Song Cartunes." In October of that same year, the Fleischers introduced a new series called "Talkartoons". Earlier entries in the series were mostly one–shot cartoons, but a new character, Bimbo became a staple of the series.

Bimbo, however, was upstaged by his girlfriend, Betty Boop, who quickly became the studio's star. Betty was the first featured female character in American animation and reflected the studio's distinctive urban adult perspective.

The Fleischers' success was further solidified when they licensed Popeye the Sailor for a cartoon series of his own. Popeye eventually became the most popular series the Fleischers ever produced, its success rivaling Mickey Mouse. Three Technicolor Popeye featurettes were produced in the late 1930s, which were extremely successful and were billed in many theatres alongside with or above the main feature.

In the mid–1930s, the studio's fortunes began to turn. In 1934, the Hays Code was enacted in Hollywood, which translated into severe censorship for the film industry. As a result, Betty was desexualized and much of her charm was lost.

(One might argue that in the end it was Will Hays who took Betty's "boop–oop–a–doop" away.) Even worse, the Fleischers caved in to pressure from their distributor, Paramount Pictures, to begin emulating the cutesy style of Walt Disney, which robbed the Fleischers of their distinctive edgy flavor. The most notable example of the Fleischers' adaptation of the Disney style were their Color Classics, which were essentially a copy of Disney's oh so treacly Silly Symphonies.

Fleischer's efforts to emulate Disney culminated in the production of animated feature films, following the success of Disney's Snow White and the Seven Dwarfs (1937). Paramount loaned Fleischer the money for a larger studio, which was built in Miami, Florida in order to take advantage of tax breaks and to break up union activity resulting from a bitter 1937 strike. The new Fleischer studio opened in October 1938, and production on the first feature, "Gulliver's Travels" began.

Upon its 1939 release, Gulliver performed modestly, although many felt that the quality of story and animation was far behind that of Snow White. Between the release of Gulliver and the follow–up feature "Mr. Bug Goes to Town" (1941), the Fleischers produced their best work, a series of high quality shorts starring Superman. The first short in the series, simply titled Superman, had a budget of $100,000, one of the highest ever for a theatrical short. It was nominated for an Academy Award.

Unfortunately, this late success did not help the studio's finances. The expanded staff of the new Miami studio created a high overhead, necessitating steady production. A number of the shorts turned out during this period, such as the continuing Popeye shorts and a 1941 adaptation of Raggedy Ann and Andy, maintained a high level of quality. Others, like the Stone Age shorts, and the various Gulliver spin–off series, were among the studio's least successful.

As profits dwindled, the Fleischers had to continuously request loans from Paramount, putting more and more of the shares of their studio up as collateral. In addition, Max and Dave Fleischer were no longer on speaking terms. Paramount had both Fleischers submit a signed letter of resignation, to be used at Paramount's discretion, in order for the Fleischer Studio to receive financing for the 1940–1941 film season. On May 24, 1941, Paramount assumed full ownership of Fleischer Studios, Inc., and incorporated a new company, Famous Studios, as the successor to Fleischer Studios, which remained active as a corporate shell. The Fleischers remained in control of production through the end of 1941.

Mr. Bug Goes to Town was finally released on December 4, 1941. Unfortunately, Mr. Bug, unlike Gulliver, failed to make an impression of any kind, and sunk quickly. This may be partly due to the misfortune of its release date occurring just a few days before the attack on Pearl Harbor.

Dave Fleischer left the studio at that time to become the head of Columbia's Screen Gems animation studio in California. With the co–owner of their animation studio now working for a competitor, Paramount produced the letters of resignation and called their loan, bankrupting Fleischer Studios, Inc. and officially removing the Fleischers from control.

Max Fleischer went on to become an employee of the Handy studio, and Isadore Sparber, Dan Gordon, and Max Fleischer's son–in–law Seymour Kneitel became the new heads of the studio, which was moved from Miami back to New York by 1943. The Fleischers were never a major force in the industry again, but their films and characters have remained popular, and today, the Fleischers are recognized as the animation pioneers that they were.

MAX FLEISCHER – Gurus and Philosophers

- Betty Boop
- Bimbo
- Bluto
- Color Classics
- Gabby
- Grampy
- Gulliver's Travels
- J. Wellington Wimpy
- Koko the Clown
- Mister Bug Goes to Town
- Olive Oyl
- Out of the Inkwell
- Poopdeck Pappy
- Popeye the Sailor
- Screen Songs
- Superman
- Swee' Pea
- Talkartoons

FRED LADD (EARLY ANIMÈ)

Fred Ladd, a native of Toledo, Ohio, did not start out in animation. His involvement was, in fact, somewhat serendipitous.

"I had gone to work at an advertising agency," he recalls, "where I wound up doing a lot of nature documentaries. The very first one, "Jungle," was about animals and their natural habitats. It was sold to some countries which could not export dollars to pay for the shows, but they could send us films in exchange.

"So, the question became, 'What kind of film are we going to take?' We didn't want to have foreign art films—we weren't in that business—but there were a lot of cartoons that we could take," which they did. Ladd thus took on the task of adapting these films for the American market.

His solution was to dub them into English and package them into 5 to 5–1/2 minute episodes, which were released under the name of Cartoon Classics. His success with this and two other programs, The Space Explorers and The New Adventurers of the Space Explorer, led to his involvement in the production of the animated feature, Pinocchio in Outer Space, which was released theatrically by Universal Pictures.

Astroboy

"Sometime in 1963," Ladd recalls, "NBC's representative in Tokyo saw a very, very limited action, adventure show on television about a little boy called Tetsuan Atom, which means Iron Fisted Atom Boy. NBC picked it up very cheap, not even knowing what they were buying. No one spoke Japanese. No one really understood it."

"They then tracked me down, knowing I had done a lot of cartoon dubbing as well as Pinocchio in Outer Space, and showed me a couple of episodes and asked me what I thought. As a result, I made a pilot, NBC saw it and said, 'Alright, do another one. We think we can sell this'. I did and it became Astroboy ."

Over the next two years, Ladd prepared 104 episodes of the show for the American market. The show was not shown on network television, but was marketed via syndication and sold to some 50 stations around the country, where it proved to be very successful.

"Astroboy ," Ladd points out, "was created by Osamu Tezuka, who was known as the Walt Disney of Japan. Tetsuan Atom had appeared first on the Fuji Television Network, which had just started up, and transmitted only in black and white, which is why the show was produced that way. "The show," he feels, "put Japan on the map as an animation production country. And as soon as that hit, all of a sudden, all over Tokyo, a hundred studios sprang up overnight."

Gigantor & Kimba

In 1964, an agent came to NBC Enterprises "with another Japanese show, Tetsujin 28 (Iron Man 28), about a giant robot in the year 2000 and beyond. But NBC passed on it, as they did not want to compete with themselves." However, they referred him to Ladd, who bought the show, which became Gigantor. It was distributed by Trans-Lux and "became a big hit."

"In 1965," Ladd recalls, "Tezuka's company came out with its first color production, Jungle Taitei (Jungle Emperor), which became Kimba, the White Lion and was again handled by NBC. In the original show, the lion was called Leo; we almost called him Simba, but Kimba was a unique word, Simba was not."

"Kimba went to 52 episodes. More were made in Japan, but NBC didn't commit to them. They just took the shows where Kimba was a cuddly little white lion, not the ones where he becomes an adult. They just wanted him to stay a little lion, as Bambi was a cute little deer."

Like the previous Japanese shows he worked on, Kimba proved to be a "big money maker" in the US. Years later, it gained a bit of unintended fame when Disney was accused by animé fans of basing much of The Lion King on the show. Ladd recalls noting the many "coincidences" between the two when he first saw the Disney film. "Finally, after five or six striking similarities, there was a pan up to the sky. I said to my wife, 'Don't tell me that the father lion is going to appear in the clouds. And he did! I couldn't believe it!"

He feels that Disney's assertion at the time that no one on The Lion King had been influenced by Kimba was ludicrous. However, he notes that, "Tezuka was a big fan of Disney. In fact, Tezuka did a 45 minute featurette in which he used characters that looked like the seven dwarfs. So, when Disney proved to be an admirer of Kimba, the studio did not retaliate.

Speed Racer

Ladd continued working on various Japanese series, including doing the "early work," for the English–language versions of Speed Racer. His most recent project was helping put together the American version of Sailor Moon for DiC.

FRED LADD – *Gurus and Philosophers*

- Astroboy
- Kimba the White Lion
- Gigantor
- Eighth Man
- Speed Racer

HANNA–BARBERA

The careers of comedy writer Bill Hanna and cartoonist Joe Barbera merged in 1940, when both were working in the Cartoon Department at MGM. Their first joint effort was a Tom and Jerry cartoon entitled, "Puss Gets the Boot" (1940). Dozens of Tom and Jerry episodes were to follow. When the studio closed its cartoon unit nearly two decades later, the two decided to try their hands at television.

In 1957, armed with their reputations from film, the pair successfully approached Columbia's Screen Gems television studio with a storyboard for Ruff and Reddy, a cartoon tale about two pals—a dog and a cat.

The ensuing success of Ruff and Reddy as wrap-around segments for recycled movie cartoons (including Tom and Jerry) proved to be the beginning of a lengthy career in television animation. In late 1958, Hanna and Barbera launched Huckleberry Hound, the first cartoon series to receive an Emmy award. This half-hour syndicated program featured, in addition to the title character, such cartoon favorites as Yogi Bear, Pixie and Dixie, Augie Doggie, and Quick Draw McGraw.

In 1960, when a survey revealed that more than half of Huckleberry Hound's audience were adults, Hanna and Barbera turned their efforts toward creating a cartoon for prime time. The result was The Flintstones, a series that drew on and parodied conventions of popular live-action domestic sitcoms—most specifically in this case Jackie Gleason's The Honeymooners. The comical premise of a "typical" suburban family living in a cartoon "Stone Age," with home appliances represented as talking animals and frequent celebrity guest stars enabled The Flintstones to attract both child and adult audiences during its initial run on ABC (1960–66). The Jetsons, a "space-age" counterpart to The Flintstones, joined its predecessor in prime time in 1962.

Unlike The Flintstones, The Jetsons would last only one season in ABC's evening schedule. However, in the late 1960s both programs became extremely popular in Saturday morning cartoon line-ups and subsequently in syndication. The programs were so successful as reruns that in the 1980s, 51 new episodes of The Jetsons were produced, as were TV specials and movies based on both The Flintstones and The Jetsons. Flintstones spin-off series for children-including Pebbles and Bamm-Bamm (1971-72 and 1975-76), The Flintstones Comedy Hour (1972-74), and The Flintstones Kids (1986-90)-have also appeared since the original series ceased production.

Other popular Hanna-Barbera series have included children's cartoons such as "Scooby-Doo, Where Are You!" (1969), plus a number of subsequent Scooby-Doo series, The Smurfs-a concept based on a Belgian cartoon series and first brought to Hanna-Barbera by network executive Fred Silverman (1981), "Pac-Man" (1982), "Pound Puppies-" (1986), and "Captain Planet" (1994). As of the 1990s, Hanna-Barbera Productions, now a subsidiary of Turner Broadcasting System, boasted a library of several thousand cartoon episodes.

HANNA-BARBERA – *Gurus and Philosophers*

- 1957 Ruff and Reddy
- 1958 Huckleberry Hound
- 1959 Quick Draw McGraw
- 1960 The Flintstones
- 1960 Snagglepuss
- 1961 The Yogi Bear Show
- 1961 Top Cat
- 1962 The Jetsons
- 1964 Jonny Quest
- 1967 Fantastic Four
- 1969 Scooby Doo
- 1971 Pebbles and Bamm-Bamm
- 1972 The Flintstones Comedy Hour
- 1973 Yogi's Gang
- 1973 Superfriends
- 1978 The New Fantastic Four
- 1981 The Smurfs
- 1982 Pac-Man
- 1985 The Jetsons
- 1985 Funtastic World of Hanna Barbera
- 1986 Pound Puppies
- 1986 The Flintstone Kids

- 1987 Snorks
- 1987 Sky Commanders
- 1987 Popeye and Son
- 1993 Captain Planet
- 1994 The New Adventures of Captain Planet

JAY WARD PRODUCTIONS

It isn't often that a career in real estate leads to a career in animation, but that's how it worked out for Jay Ward. When, in 1947 Ward's friend, Alexander Anderson Jr., decided to enter the burgeoning field of television, the main reason he approached Ward as a business partner was because Ward, having succeeded in his first career, had money.

Anderson had already been turned down by animation mogul Paul Terry (his uncle, incidentally). Never an innovator, Terry saw no reason to seek out a new market – the old one, neighborhood movie theaters, was a fine place to sell cartoons.

Ward brought more than mere investment capital to the table. He became intimately involved with development and production. When their first cartoon (titled "The Comic Strips of Television") was broadcast in 1948, it was at least as much Ward's creation as Anderson's.

"The Comic Strips of Television" was a vehicle for test–marketing some of the characters they'd come up with – Crusader Rabbit, Ham hock Jones and Dudley Do–Right. Nothing was ever done with Ham hock Jones, and Dudley Do– Right stayed on the shelf until 1961, but Crusader Rabbit went

Everything I need to know, I learned from Cartoons!

into regular production. Though the networks all turned it down, it was sold on a city–by–city basis, and was aired in some areas as early as 1949. It was the first animated series to debut on TV.

The Crusader Rabbit property was eventually sold to other producers, and Anderson got out of the animation business. Ward retained ownership of everything the studio had in development, including an animated ensemble show based in the mythical town of Frostbite Falls, Minnesota. That one eventually metamorphosed into Rocky& His Friends, which debuted on NBC in 1959.

Excellence in animation was never the studio's strong point. Crusader Rabbit was virtually nothing but a series of still drawings, and Bullwinkle never won any prizes for production either. What made them stand out was their wit.

Ward strove to reach three audiences – pre–verbal youngsters, who could enjoy the sounds and colors; kids who could appreciate a storyline with fast–moving events piled one on top of another; and adults, for whom the clever wordplay and wry commentary were intended. He succeeded on all levels – not so well that the shows were wildly popular, like some of the contemporary Hanna–Barbera productions, but quite enough to develop a loyal following.

By the time Rocky debuted, Ward had been joined by Bill Scott as co–producer. Scott, whose animation credits go back to the early 1940s, had left United Productions of America, where he'd done significant work on both Mr. Magoo and Gerald McBoing–Boing, in the midst of the McCarthy–inspired zeal to purge the entertainment industry of that era's perception of political incorrectitude. UPA's loss was Ward's gain, as Scott didn't just punch up scripts with his zany sense of humor – he also provided some of the studio's best voices (including those of Bullwinkle, George of the Jungle and many of the male characters in Peabody's Improbable History and Fractured Fairy Tales). (On the credits of the cartoons, however, the producer was listed as "Ponsonby Britt, O.B.E.," an entirely fictitious personage.)

Jay Ward Productions continued turning out fabulously inventive cartoons for the next few years. While its following was enthusiastic, it was not, by network television standards, very large. Series proposals such as "Fang the Wonder Dog" and "Hawkear" (about an Indian scout of the Old West) went unproduced, because the networks wouldn't accept them without massive changes. The studio came to rely more and more on its commercial work, particularly for Quaker cereals – first, with its regular characters acting as spokestoons for existing products, and later with new products based on Ward–designed characters (such as Quisp, Quake and Cap'n Crunch).

JAY WARD – Gurus and Philosophers

- "Crusader Rabbit" (1949)
- "Rocky and His Friends" (1959)
- "The Bullwinkle Show" (1961)
- "Fractured Flickers" (1963)
- "Hoppity Hooper" (1964)
- "Uncle Waldo's Cartoon Show" (1966)
- "George of the Jungle" (1967)

KING FEATURES

Founded in 1915 to manage and collect royalties for the comics in William Randolph Hearst's newspapers, King Features Syndicate is today the world's premier distributor of comics, columns, editorial cartoons, puzzles, and games to newspapers. The list of characters they license is astounding, and as a very small sampling includes Blondie, Dennis the Menace, Hagar the Horrible, and Popeye

In 1962, King Features created a half-hour, made-for-tv, cartoon trilogy featuring Beetle Bailey, Snuffy Smith and Krazy Kat. Seymour Kneitel (of Famous Studios) directed Beetle and Snuffy. Gene Deitch (of Terrytoons) directed Krazy Kat. The series aired in 1963.

KING FEATURES TRILOGY – *Gurus and Philosophers*

- Beetle Bailey
- Snuffy Smith
- Krazy Kat

TERRYTOONS

Paul Terry, founder of Terrytoons, became interested in animation in 1914 when, as a newspaper photographer in New York City, he attended one of cartoonist Winsor McCay's early showings of Gertie the Dinosaur. A year later, he'd produced an entire animated short, Little Hermann, single-handed but had trouble selling it to distributors for as much as he'd spent on the film to make it.

He did, however, manage to get an operation rolling, and began producing a monthly short for John R. Bray's screen magazine, Paramount Pictograph (which also distributed the Fleischer Studio's series, "Out of the Inkwell").

Farmer Alfalfa, the character Terry used in these cartoons, served Terry for decades, remaining a star until the late 1930s and being used as a supporting character well into the '50s. Terry went through several financial backers and several distributors, finally settling, in 1938, on releasing his cartoons through 20th Century Fox.

Terry was an early user of the cell method of animation, which enabled animators to use richly textured backgrounds (since they didn't have to be redrawn for each frame). But the enhanced quality wasn't why he went for it – he was more interested in its labor-saving ability, and was a pioneer in animating different parts of the body on different cells, because it saved time and therefore money.

And saving money was what kept Terry's studio alive while others came and went. He was not an artistic innovator, but he was able to turn out cartoons reliably, on a regular basis, without exceeding his meager budgets. He adopted technological advances, such as sound and color, when it became necessary to do so for continued survival, but not one minute sooner. "Disney is the Tiffany's in this business," he was often heard to remark, "and I am the Woolworth's."

Terrytoons became a byword in the industry for bargain–basement animation, turning out cartoons like yard goods. And yet, some of the studio's output transcended its lowly origin. The Gandy Goose cartoons were often charmingly whimsical. Oil Can Harry, the villain in a series of opera–style "mellerdramas," is fondly recalled even today though more for his 1940s–50s association with Mighty Mouse than for the 1930s black–and–whites in which he originally appeared. The Heckle & Jekyll series was basically a good idea – incredibly obnoxious identical twins – and their cartoons were occasionally quite funny. Four Terrytoons were actually nominated for Academy Awards – "All Out for V" (1942), "My Boy, Johnny" (1944), "Mighty Mouse in Gypsy Life" (1945) and Sidney the Elephant in "Sidney's Family Tree" (1958). None, however, actually won the Oscar.

As cost–conscious as Terry was, it's surprising he didn't pursue the potential revenues of licensing more assiduously than he did. Other than comic books (licensed first to Marvel Comics in 1942 and later to St. John, Pines, Dell and Gold Key before ending in the mid-'60s), there was very little marketing of Terrytoons properties outside of the cartoons themselves.

One thing Terrytoons had going for it was employee loyalty. Many talented animators and story men simply passed through on the way to something better, including Bill Tytla (who animated Tchernobog, the demon in Fantasia), Dan Gordon (later credited with creating The Flintstones), Joe Barbera (of Hanna-Barbera) ... but those who stuck around, stuck around. Animators and directors like Connie Rasinski, Mannie Davis, Eddie Donnelly and many more spent their careers at Terrytoons, creating a kind of family atmosphere. This contributed to stagnation in the product, (Terrytoons of the early 1950s looked very much like those of the late '30s, when they first went to color), but it also contributed to the blunting of unionization attempts in the 1940s.

Imagine the employees' surprise, then, when, in 1955, Terry suddenly sold the operation to CBS and retired with millions, leaving them flat. He lived another 16 years in luxurious indolence, while his formerly loyal staff labored under a new regime that might well be described as stressful.

CBS brought in Gene Deitch, late of UPA, to head the studio. Veterans with decades in the business, suddenly found themselves taking orders from a 31-year-old hotshot, loaded with new ideas.

Deitch brought in not just a new look, but also new characters. Clint Clobber, Gaston LeCrayon, John Doormat, et al. replaced Dinky Duck, The Terry Bears, Little Roquefort and their contemporaries. Also, new characters, like Tom Terrific, which many consider the best of the Deitch–era Terrytoons, were seen only on television.

Deitch was gone after two years, but the new budgets remained – and so did most of the staff. But a younger crew began to come aboard, most notably Ralph Bakshi, better known for his later work as an independent producer (it was he who brought R. Crumb's Fritz the Cat to the big screen). Bakshi became a Terrytoons animator in 1959, when he was 21, and a director in 1963. He worked on many series, for both theatrical release and TV, including Deputy Dawg and Sad Cat, but his best–known work there is a superhero spoof titled The Mighty Heroes.

TERRYTOONS (Television) – Gurus and Philosophers
- Heckle and Jekyll
- Mighty Mouse
- Oil Can Harry
- Dinky
- Little Roquefort
- Deputy Dawg

TRANS–LUX

Trans–Lux, which distributed Felix the Cat, Speed Racer and others was primarily a manufacturer of real–time displays, becoming known for their stock market tickers.

The company began as "Edison Electric Industries," a subsidiary of the group of companies owned by Thomas Edison. Among several products introduced by Trans–Lux was the first stock ticker display technology used in the New York Stock Exchange. Implemented in 1923, this device took information from a stock ticker, printed it on clear motion picture film stock, and then displayed that information on a wall using a projector. Before Trans–Lux, stock summary information had to be hand–written, usually on a chalk board, so this was a vast improvement. It is this stock ticker device that gave the company its name. ("Trans–Lux" means "moving light").

Over the years, Trans–Lux dabbled in other lines of work that had seemingly little to do with display technology. Among them, running a movie theater chain, distributing films such as "The African Queen," and running a television program syndication service, which is ultimately how they got into cartoons.

TRANS–LUX – Gurus and Philosophers
- Felix the Cat
- Gigantor (with Fred Ladd)

- Speed Racer (with Fred Ladd)
- Hercules

UPA

UPA was founded in the wake of the Disney animators' strike of 1941, which resulted in a number of long–time Disney employees leaving the studio. One of the animators taking part in the Disney exodus was John Hubley, an artist who disagreed with the ultra–realistic style of animation that Disney had developed. Along with a number of other animators, Hubley promoted the idea that animation did not have to be a painstakingly realistic imitation of real life.

After leaving Disney, Hubley worked together with animators Zack Schwartz, Dave Hilberman and Steve Bosustow to form a studio called first United Film Production and later Industrial Films and Poster Service, where they were able to apply their ideas of animation. Finding work (and income) in the then booming field of wartime work for the government, the small studio produced a cartoon sponsored by the United Auto Workers (UAW) in 1944. This cartoon was entitled "Hell–Bent for Election" (directed by Chuck Jones), a film made for the re-election campaign of Franklin D. Roosevelt. The film was a major theatrical success, and with its sudden fame, the studio re-named itself United Productions of America (UPA). Another notable UPA effort was Brotherhood of Man (1946), which was again sponsored by the UAW. The film, directed by Bob Cannon preached tolerance of all people, regardless of their ethnic background. The short was groundbreaking, not only in its message but in its very flat, stylized design that completely defied the Disney approach that dominated the 1930s.

Initially, UPA contracted with the government to produce animation, but the government contracts quickly evaporated when the FBI began investigating suspected Communist activities in Hollywood in the late 1940s. No formal charges were filed against anyone at UPA, but the government contracts were quickly cancelled as Washington severed its ties with Hollywood.

UPA moved to the crowded field of theatrical cartoons to sustain itself, and quickly won a contract with Columbia Pictures to try to breathe life into their moribund cartoon studio. Columbia's Screen Gems cartoon studio had been uniformly unexceptional since the heyday of Krazy Kat in the silent era. The UPA animators applied their ideas of animation to Columbia's theatrical cartoons, working with their characters The Fox and the Crow. Robin Hoodlum (1948), the first UPA effort for Columbia was so successful that it earned the studio an Academy Award nomination. Another highly- successful short produced for Columbia during the late 1940s was The Ragtime Bear (1949), the first appearance of Mr. Magoo. Bear was a box-office hit, and UPA's star quickly rose as the 1950s dawned.

As one of the few "human" cartoon characters in a Hollywood full of talking mice, rabbits, and bears, as well as having a unique, simplistic drawing style that contrasted greatly with other cartoons of the day, the Mr. Magoo series won accolades for UPA and made the competing animation studios sit up and take notice. Two Magoo cartoons won the Academy Award for Best Short Subject (Cartoons): "When Magoo Flew" in 1953 and "Magoo's Puddle Jumper" in 1955.

In 1951, UPA scored another major hit with "Gerald McBoing–Boing", based on a story by Dr. Seuss. "Gerald McBoing–Boing" won UPA another Academy Award. Several UPA cartoons would receive Oscar nominations in the next few years. With such cartoons as "The Tell–Tale Heart" and "Rooty Toot Toot" taking risks and offering the public something different from cat–mouse battles and Silly Symphonies, UPA's unique style of limited animation struck the industry of theatrical cartoons like a lightning bolt. It influenced style changes in all of the other major animation studios, including Warner Bros., MGM, and even the industry giant, Disney. The days of lush, painstakingly–detailed animation came to an end, but they were replaced by a new era of experimentation and artistic growth, which, unfortunately, did not last very long.

The HUAC commission hearings on Communism in Hollywood took a heavy toll on UPA, because many members of its animation staff had been free–thinking, independent artists who had supported controversial ideas. This caused difficulty for Columbia Pictures, and in 1952 John Hubley was blacklisted and let go from his position at UPA. When he left, much of the innovation and creativity of UPA left with him. The studio continued under the guidance of Bosustow, but the energetic, innovative quality of UPA's cartoons quickly faded.

As the major Hollywood studios began cutting back and shutting down their animation studios with the dawn of the 1960s, UPA was in financial straits, and Steve Bosustow sold the studio to a new producer, Henry G. Saperstein. Saperstein turned UPA's focus to television to sustain itself. This proved to be a death–knell for the studio, for though it was able to produce income by expanding the Mr. Magoo series and bringing it to television, the quality of the series faded and became a shadow of its former self. UPA produced other animated series for TV, including an adaptation of the comic strip Dick Tracy, but the rigors of television snuffed out UPA's flame. UPA was forced to churn out cartoons at a far greater quantity than the studio had done for theatrical release; this caused the Mr. Magoo series to sink to an embarrassing level.

The UPA style of limited animation was adopted by other animation studios, and especially by TV cartoon studios such as Hanna–Barbera Productions. However, this was done as a cost–cutting measure rather than as an art form. This was in spite of the fact that UPA's pioneering of the form was meant to expand the boundaries of animation and create a new form of art.

One bright moment in the UPA television era came with "Mr. Magoo's Christmas Carol" (1963), the first episode of an animated TV series entitled "The Famous Adventures of Mr. Magoo." Christmas Carol captured the spirit of Charles Dickens' tale in a manner that few of the many re–tellings of the story would, and it is considered to be a holiday classic of the 1960s, ranking alongside "A Charlie Brown Christmas" and "How the Grinch Stole Christmas!"

UPA (television) – Gurus and Philosophers

- Mr. Magoo
- Gerald McBoing-Boing
- Dick Tracy
- Fox and the Crow

CURLY-Q'S ™

In addition to my Kartoon-Karetakers, I was fortunate to have had three additional cartoon role-models (albeit live action cartoons). Their names were Moe, Larry and Curly. Throughout my formative years, I spent many a wistful moment pondering their wise and inscrutable lessons. The delicate sensitivies which I garnered from them cannot be overestimated.

In homage to these esoteric Zen masters, I've distilled their wisdom into Haikus, which I collectively call: "Curly-Qs." May they bring you a wealth of tranquility and comfort.

Howard! Fine! Howard!
Stooges due in surgery.
Woo, woo, woo, woo woo.

Two fingers; a poke.
Then a crowbar on my head.
Why is life so hard?

Got toimites, lady?
Relax. We'll fix your problem.
Oh boy! Woistcheshire.

You look like Hitler.
I guess that makes me Goering.
So, who's Larry then?

Got Cheese? I need some.
Or Else I'll throw a table.
Moe! Larry! The Cheese!

One day, when I'm gone,
Many will try to fill in.
The worst? Joe Besser.

Shaddup chowderhead!
Or I'll tear your tonsils out–
To make a bow–tie.

If you love me dear,
Free me from the cider–press
I'll never be juice.

His hair is bowl–cut.
His, like a porcupine – wild.
I've no hair. Slap me.

You fed me a bone.
It hurt my toothie–woothie.
A door–knob's the cure.

INDEX

A

Aesop & Son, 63
Alvin, 10
Archie, 11, 65, 98
Arnold Stang, 78
Art Clokey, 36
Asgaard, 76
Astro, 44
Astroboy, 12, 35, 104, 105, 107
Atom Ant, 63
Augie Doggie, 59, 108
Aunt May, 72

B

B. B. Eyes, 24
Baba Booey, 59
Baba Looey, 58
Baby Huey, 97
Bamm–Bamm, 32, 109
Barbara Holmes, 3
Barbera, 25, 39, 46, 52, 58, 63, 64, 65, 67, 82, 85, 99, 107, 108, 109, 111, 116, 122
Barney, 68
Barney Rubble, 31, 68
Bart, 89
Bart Simpson, 88
Batman, 21, 98
Battyman, 81
Beany and Cecil, 13, 14
Beavis and Butthead, 92
Bedrock, 31
Beetle Bailey, 15, 69, 113
Benny the Ball, 78
Betty Boop, 15, 53, 54, 99, 100, 103
Betty Rubble, 31
Bill Cosby, 28
Bill Gates, 83
Bill Scott, 32, 50, 61, 111
Bill Tytla, 116
Blondie, 113
Blossom, 90
Bluto, 54, 103
Bob Clampett, 13
Bob Kane, 21
Boo–Boo, 85

Boris Badenov, 62
Boris Godunov, 62
Boy Gary, 59
Bozo the Clown, 97
Breezly & Sneezly, 53
Bruce Banner, 41
Bubbles, 90
Bugs Bunny, 16, 37, 61
Bullwinkle, 17, 26, 32, 51, 60, 61, 62, 63, 111, 112
Burl Ives, 92
Buttercup, 90

C

Captain America, 18, 41, 42, 74, 76
Captain Kangaroo, 77
Captain Kidney Bean, 77
Captain Planet, 96, 109, 110
Care Bears, 96
Cartman, 93
Casper, 19, 97
Charlie Brown, 51, 52, 123
Chef, 93
Chief Fumblethumbs, 27
Choo Choo, 78
Chuck Jones, 16, 60, 61, 119
Chumley, 75
Clyde Crashcup, 10
Cocoa Puffs, 20
Commander McBragg, 75
Cosmo and Wanda, 86
Cosmo G. Spacely, 43
Courageous Cat, 21
Coyote, 60, 80
Crabby Appleton, 77
Crusader Rabbit, 110, 111, 112

D

Dave Fleischer, 53, 99, 102
Dave Seville, 10
Daws Butler, 18, 40, 52, 58, 60, 82
Dennis the Menace, 96, 113
Deputy Dawg, 21, 117
Deva Brown, 3
DiC Entertainment, 96
Dick Dastardly, 22
Dick Tracy, 24, 122, 123

Dimmsdale, 86
Dishonest John, 14
Disney, 30, 34, 96, 97, 99, 100, 101, 105, 106, 107, 115, 119, 121
DoDo – the kid from outer space, 25
Don Adams, 74
Dr. Brilliant, 35
Dr. Packadermus J. Elefun, 12
Dr. Seuss, 33, 34, 121
Dudley Do–Right, 26, 63, 110
Dum Dum, 82
Dumb Donald, 29

E

Edward Everett Horton, 63
Edward G. Robinson, 21
Eep Opp Ork Ah ah, 44
Eighth Man, 27, 35, 107
El Kabong, 59
Elroy, 44
Elzie Segar, 53
Eugene the Jeep, 54

F

Fairly Odd Parents, 86
Famous Studios, 19, 56, 97, 102, 113
Fancy Fancy, 78
Fang the Wonder Dog, 112
Fantasia, 116
Fantastic Four, 74
Farmer Alfalfa, 114
Fat Albert, 28, 98
Fearless Leader, 62
Felix, 29, 30, 118
Felix the Cat, 29, 118
Filmation, 11, 28, 97, 98
Flattop, 24
Fleischer, 15, 53, 55, 56, 97, 99, 101, 102, 103, 114
Flintstone Kids, 109
Flintstones, 31, 44, 108, 109, 116
Fox and the Crow, 34, 120, 123
Fractured Fairy Tales, 63, 112
Fred Flintstone, 31
Fred Ladd, 35, 104, 107, 118, 119
Fritz the Cat, 117
Friz Freleng, 16
Fuzzy Lumpkins, 91

G

Gabby, 103
Gafagahaga, 93
Gandy Goose, 115
Gaston LeCrayon, 117
Gene Deitch, 37, 77, 113, 116
General Mills, 80
George Jetson, 43
George of the Jungle, 32, 79, 112
George Raft, 81
Gerald McBoing–Boing, 33, 34, 112, 121
Gertie the Dinosaur, 114
Gigantor, 35, 105, 106, 107, 118
Goering, 124
Go–Go Gomez, 24
Goldfinger, 64
Grampy, 103
Grinch, 123
Groovie Goolies, 98
Gulliver's Travels, 101
Gumby, 36

H

Hagar the Horrible, 113
Hal Sutherland, 97
Ham Gravy, 53
Ham hock Jones, 110
Hanna, 25, 39, 46, 52, 58, 63, 64, 65, 67, 82, 85, 99, 107, 108, 109, 111, 116, 122
Hanna–Barbera, 25, 46, 52, 58, 63, 64, 65, 67, 85, 99, 109, 111, 116, 122
Hardy Har Har, 82
Heap O' Calorie, 24
Heckle and Jekyll, 22, 36, 117
Hemlock Holmes, 24
Henry G. Saperstein, 122
Herbie Hancock, 28
Hercules, 38, 119
Herman and Katnip, 97
Herman's Hermits, 51
Hippo Hurricane Holler, 52
Hitler, 73, 124
Homer, 62
Homer Simpson, 62, 88
Hong Kong Phooey, 38, 39
Howard Stern, 59
Huckleberry Hound, 39, 40, 58, 84, 108, 109

Everything I need to know, I learned from Cartoons!

Hulk, 18, 41, 42, 74, 76, 96
Human Torch, 74

I

Imaginary Friends, 87, 88
Industrial Films and Poster Service, 119
Inspector Gadget, 74, 96
Iron Man, 18, 41, 42, 74, 76, 106
Isadore Sparber, 56, 97, 103
Isotope Feaney, 77
Itchy, 24

J

J. Wellington Wimpy, 103
Jack Mercer, 30, 54, 56
Jackie Gleason, 108
Jackson Beck, 54
James Bond, 64
Jane Jetson, 43
Jasmine Brown, 3
Jay Ward, 17, 32, 60, 62, 110, 112
Jean LaFoote, 17, 18
JellystonePark, 85
Jerry Lewis, 98
Jesus Christ, 93
Jetson, 43, 44
Jetsons, 43, 108, 109
Jim Backus, 49
Jimmy Durante, 59
Jimmy Sparks, 35
Jo Jitsu, 24
Joe Besser, 124
John Hubley, 49, 119, 121
John Kricfalusi, 92
John R. Bray, 114
Jorgen Von Strangle, 86
Jot, 42
Judy, 43
June Foray, 32, 61

K

Kenny, 75, 93
Kimba, 105, 106, 107
King Features, 15, 55, 68, 69, 113
King Leonardo, 75
Klondike Kat, 75
Koko the Clown, 99, 103
Krazy Kat, 15, 61, 69, 113, 120

Krishna, 40
Kyle Broslovsky, 93

L

Lariat Sam, 77
Larry Storch, 75
Lionel Barrymore, 81
Lionel Wilson, 22, 77
Lippy the Lion, 82
Lisa Simpson, 88
Little Lulu, 97
Little Roquefort, 117
Lois Lane, 81
Loki, 76
Looney Tunes, 16
Lucky Charms, 45
Lucky the Leprechaun, 45

M

Madame Foster, 87
Mae Questel, 54, 56, 83
Maggie Simpson, 88, 96
Magilla Gorilla, 46
Man from Uncle, 64
Marge Simpson, 88
Mark Twain, 60
Mary–Kate And Ashley In Action, 96
Matt Groening, 88
Matthew, 42
Max Fleischer, 15, 97, 99, 103
Mel Blanc, 24, 43, 49, 63, 79
Merrie Melodies, 16
Merry Marvel Marching Society, 18, 41, 73, 76
MGM, 107, 121
Mickey Mouse, 30, 54, 100
Mighty Heroes, 117
Mighty Manfred the Wonder Dog, 77
Mighty Mouse, 48, 98, 115, 117
Minute Mouse, 21
Moe, Larry and Curly, 124
Mojo Jojo, 91
Monroe Mann, 3
Morocco Mole, 64
Mr. Big, 62
Mr. Bug Goes to Town, 101, 102
Mr. Eugene H. Krabs, 94
Mr. Hanky, 93
Mr. Magoo, 49, 112, 120, 121, 122, 123

Mr. Peabody, 50
Mr. Spacely, 43
Mrs. Broslovsky, 93
Mumbles, 24
Mushmouse, 46
Mushmouth, 29
Muskie the Muskrat, 22
Muttley, 23, 44

N

Natasha, 62
Nell Fenwick, 26
Nickelodeon, 92
Noodles, 24
Norman Prescott, 97

O

Odin, 76
Officer Dibble, 78
Ogee, 47
Oil Can Harry, 115, 117
Olive Oyl, 53, 54, 56, 103
Osamu Tezuka, 105
Otto Messmer, 29
Out of the Inkwell, 99, 103, 114
Overcat, 81

P

Park Ranger Smith, 85
Pat Sullivan, 29
Patrick Star, 94
Paul Frees, 32, 64, 79
Paul McCartney, 89
Paul Terry, 48, 110, 114
Paul Winchell, 22
Pebbles, 32, 109
Penelope Pitstop, 22
Peter Lorre, 64
Peter Noone, 51
Peter Parker, 72
Peter Potamus, 52
Phil Silvers, 78
Phineas J. Whoopee, 75
Phooeymobile, 39
Pinto Colvig, 54
Pip–Eye, 55
Pixie and Dixie, 108
Poindexter, 30
Pokey, 36

Ponsonby Britt, O.B.E., 112
Poopdeck Pappy, 54, 103
Poop–Eye, 55
Popeye, 30, 53, 54, 55, 56, 97, 99, 100, 102, 103, 110, 113
Pottsylvania, 62
Pound Puppies, 109
Powerpuff Girls, 90, 91
Prince Namor, 73
Professor Genius, 27, 35
Professor Utonium, 90
Professor Very, Very Smart, 27
Pruneface, 24
Pup–Eye, 55

Q

Quake, 60, 112
Quick Draw McGraw, 58, 59, 108, 109
Quisp, 60, 112

R

Ralph Bakshi, 117
Ren, 92
Ricochet Rabbit, 46
Riff Raff, 81
Road Runner, 60, 61
Robert McKimson, 16
Rock Bottom, 30
Rocky, 26, 32, 51, 60, 61, 62, 111, 112
Ronald Coleman, 79
Ross Bagdasarian, 10
Ruff and Reddy, 39, 108, 109
Rugrats, 92

S

Sabrina, the Teenage Witch, 98
Sad Cat, 117
Sailor Moon, 96, 107
Sandy Cheeks, 94
Santa Claus, 93
Saucer Lip, 27
Scatman Crothers, 39
Scooby–Doo, 44, 64, 65, 109
Secret Squirrel, 63, 64
Semour Kneitel, 113
Sergeant Snorkle, 15
Seymour Kneitel, 56, 97, 103
Shaggy, 65
Sheldon J. Plankton, 94

Everything I need to know, I learned from Cartoons!

Shep, 32
Sherman, 50, 51, 63
Shoeshine Boy, 81
Sidney the Elephant, 22, 115
Silly Symphonies, 101, 121
Simon Bar Sinister, 81
Simpsons, 88, 89
Sketch Paree, 24
Smurfs, 66, 96, 109
Snagglepuss, 84, 109
Snidely Whiplash, 23, 26
Snooper and Blabber, 59
Snowball II, 88
Snuffy Smith, 15, 68, 113
Sonny the Cuckoo Bird, 20
So–So the monkey, 52
SouthPark, 93
Speed Racer, 25, 69, 70, 107, 118, 119
Spider Man, 71
SpongeBob, 94
Squidward Q. Tentacles, 94
Stanley Livingston, 75
Star Trek, 98
Stimpson J. Cat, 92
Stimpy, 92
Submariner, 18, 41, 73, 76
Super Mario, 96
Superman, 38, 48, 56, 81, 91, 97, 98, 99, 101, 103
Superwitch, 98
Sweet Polly Purebred, 81
Sweet Tooth Sam, 77

T

Talkartoons, 100, 103
Tchernobog, 116
Tennessee Tuxedo, 74
Terrytoons, 36, 37, 77, 113, 114, 115, 116, 117
Tetsuan Atom, 105
Tetsujin 28, 106
Tex Avery, 34
The Brow, 24
The Comic Strips of Television, 110
The Electric Eel, 81
The Gruesome Twosome, 22
The Junkyard Gang, 28
The Mole, 24
The Smurfs, 66, 96, 109
The Yellow Pinkie, 64

Thimble Theatre, 53
Thor, 18, 41, 42, 76
Tobor, 27
Tom and Jerry, 61, 98, 107, 108
Tom Terrific, 22, 77, 117
Tony Stark, 41, 42
Tooky–Tooky bird, 33
Top Cat, 78, 109
Toucan Sam, 79
Touché Turtle, 82
Trans–Lux, 38, 70, 106, 118
Trix Rabbit, 80

U

Uncle Ben, 72
Underdog, 81, 82
United Productions of America, 34, 111, 119
UPA, 33, 34, 49, 112, 116, 119, 120, 121, 122, 123

V

Veronica, 11
Vince Guaraldi, 51
Vincent Van Gopher, 22

W

Wacky Races, 22, 23
Wally Cox, 81
Wally Gator, 82
Walt Disney, 30, 34, 99, 101, 105
Warner Bros., 16, 17, 28, 99, 121
Weird Harold, 29
Wile E. Coyote, 60, 80
William Conrad, 63
Wimpy, 103
Winky–Dink, 83
Winsor McCay, 114
Woody Woodpecker, 37

Y

Yakky Doodle, 84
Yippee, Yappee & Yahooey, 53
Yogi Bear, 84, 108, 109
Yogi Berra, 85

Everything I need to know, I learned from Cartoons!

www.ingramcontent.com/pod-product-compliance
Lightning Source LLC
LaVergne TN
LVHW091557060526
838200LV00036B/885